days
Tutti
Ma-rie
Ma-rie
Flans Ma-rie Ma-rie tempest
Adrianne Allen

Those Dancing Years

MARY ELLIS

Those Dancing Years

AN AUTOBIOGRAPHY

John Murray

For Alan

© Mary Ellis 1982

First published 1982
by John Murray (Publishers) Ltd
50 Albemarle Street, London W1X 4BD

All rights reserved
Unauthorised duplication contravenes applicable laws
Typeset by Inforum Ltd, Portsmouth
Printed in Great Britain by The Camelot Press, Southampton

British Library Cataloguing in Publication Data

Ellis, Mary
Those dancing years.
1. Ellis, Mary   2. Actresses—Great Britain
—Biography
I. Title
792′.028′0924   PN2598.E/
ISBN 0-7195-3984-6

Contents

Illustrations

LINE ILLUSTRATIONS IN TEXT

ENDPAPERS

Ivor Novello's song in his hand signed by those who took part in the Marie Tempest Golden Jubilee Matinee at Drury Lane during the run of *Glamorous Night*, 1935

ILLUSTRATION ACKNOWLEDGEMENTS

25, 26, The Raymond Mander & Joe Mitchenson Theatre Collection. 27, Photo: Dorothy Wilding. 44, 45, 46, 54, 55, 57, 58, 59, Photo: Angus McBean, Copyright: Harvard Theatre Museum. 50, Photo: Pamela Chandler. 51, 52, Photo: John Vickers. 53, Photo: Press Illustrations. 56, Photo: Camera Press Ltd. Other illustrations from the author's personal collection.

1

Overture and Beginners

For a few weeks every year I leave London to look across a valley to where a small and almost apologetic river Rhône flows glacier-grey towards Lac Leman. So today, from my balcony under the chalet roof, I see the splendid spiky bulk of the Dents du Midi, snow sprinkled, and the Muveran looking for all the world like the silhouette of a giant Queen Victoria, lying in state, her toes pointing into a cloudless sky. When the sun has set she will turn to flamingo pink – and tomorrow morning at five she will be shrouded in mist. Tomorrow is my birthday; I will be eighty. I realise that if I live twenty years more, I will have had a century and the thought excites me provided I can keep my wits.

It is apricot season in this fruit-growing valley. . . . I suppose I must begin at the beginning.

*   *   *

A tree was surely a tree? And yet here was one, pressed as flat as the daisy between the leaves of my picture book. Apricots hung golden against a cream brick wall and, when one of them fell into my hands, it was as warm as the baby chick I had been allowed to hold at Easter.

Then, that same summer, we were at Mythenstrasse, Zurich, where my father's sister, Tante Sophie, had an apartment on the second floor. The entrance hall smelled of floor polish, of kettles left on the gas too long, of a drawing-room seldom aired. The mystery and silence of that room fascinated me. Chairs stood waiting, presided over by the Grand Piano, black and menacing. Even more magical; the highly polished parquet floor, half reflecting my short legs and feet ending in white button boots, that skidded on its surface. Then Tante Sophie's flushed face bending over me to scold, and to send me back into the walled garden where the warm apricots grew on spread-eagled branches.

Easter Day, New York. The century was four years old and so was I. My father lifted me up to admire my new bonnet in the mirror; brown silky beaver with two small ostrich feather tips on top and pink ribbons under my chin; my mother smiling and happy in the mirror behind me, holding a bouquet of violets and one red rose – a token sent to her every Easter of his life by my father. My sister, Lucile, twelve, was there too, looking cross, her red hair swinging in a plait as she tossed her head like an impatient pony; and Alice, my nurse, in a starched white blouse, a small dusty black velvet bow on her greying top-knot. (It's all like a very old family photograph, fading even as I think of it.) I used to lie awake night after night to watch Alice perform the miracle of removing her dentures before she said her prayers. We shared a rather dark room in the back of the flat, overlooking a courtyard, where street musicians often brought a harp, a violin, or an accordion to play, the sound echoing against the yellow brick walls. Often I was given five cents wrapped in a wad of newspaper to throw down to one of them and would watch from the window as a dejected figure strapped the harp on his back and slouched off into the dusty city sunshine. I could not see why he should be rejected for making music; it was my first brush with a special sort of injustice, which has distressed me all my life. Whenever I see a worn-thin musician on the street corner, a cold drop on the end of his nose, fiddling with stiff fingers in a dreadful out-of-key familiarity, I know he must have, sometime, somewhere, started with a dream.

Besides learning my alphabet from Alice, complete with Irish brogue, I was happiest before bed-time, when I sat on my father's lap while he sang German folk-songs, and perhaps put a record of *Fledermaus* on the gramophone, with its great golden morning-glory horn. More exalted musical moments were when I hid under the piano and watched my mother's feet on the pedals, while the waves of the 'Liebeslied', Chopin's 'Ballades', Sinding's 'Rustle of Spring' half-drowned me and swept me along into a growing delight of *sound*. I adored my father, and was frightened if I displeased him. He was the kindest of men, but expected obedience, punctuality, and order – from everyone. My poor mother was always tidying up, and a great rush sometimes went on before he came home in the evening. Mother was an ambitious pianist but her marriage at seventeen in those Victorian days had meant she gave up everything to be with her husband. She continued to study, however, with a famous Polish pianist, Alexander Lambert, who always claimed he was my true godparent, since Mother had spent hours practising at the piano while she was pregnant with me.

My father had arrived in the United States with only a franc in his pocket; his first job was as an office-boy in a paper-mill company in the South. He literally worked his way up to becoming President of the Consolidated Paper Mills, and his spruce-forests took him as far as Maine, and to Canada where I am told a village is named after him (I haven't found it on the map!) When he came home from log-rolling in Maine, he told me wonderful tales of how the hungry bears came down into the village in winter and ate out of the dustbins. And he wore a seal-skin cap with ear-muffs, which I was allowed to try on when he came back from his icy journeys; I'm sure that this was my first sensual pleasure.

My nurse, Alice, was an ardent Roman Catholic. When I was four years old she took me with her to early Mass, smuggling me out into the chill morning, knowing my parents would disapprove. I trotted along beside her, in a sleeping city, at dawn and was over-awed by the experience in church where I had to keep very still, and watch people bending their knees and saying lots of words. But I loved the singing, and the sight of candles and the smell of incense in church always takes me back to those half-frightened early Sunday mornings when I was hustled back into bed again before the household was awake and told not to tell. It had a lasting effect on me – so much so, that years later in London I sought out a wonderful old Jesuit priest, Father Hickey, to find out all that I had missed. He tried to make me into a good Catholic – alas, without success – but even so, something came full circle.

From Alice I learned the rudiments of morality, optimism and compassion. When I saw a dead cat in the gutter and asked what had killed it, she promptly said 'Curiosity', and I was convinced that all cats died of it. When I sobbed my heart out because of some infant hurt, she clasped me to her starched bosom, and when there was a sudden sand-storm in Central Park, she rushed me home in my go-cart, full of grit from my teeth to my toes, turned me upside down and literally shook the sand out of me.

This cosiness was in direct opposition to the vague aware-ness I had of my mother. I really cannot remember her until I was about six – and Alice had gone by then, leaving me desolate. My mother was lovely to look at, and father adored her. They had had a hard time when they first married. My sister was born in Texas one very hot July day, a fiery red wisp of hair on her head. In the years before I came along my parents became more comfortably settled, and moved to New York – to the little brick house where I was born. It was hardly big enough to house Mother and Father, my mother's sister Matilda and her husband, my sister and me. As Matilda had a gorgeous voice, and Mother was an accomplished pianist, there were musical excursions in the evenings, coming back from the opera, or a concert, to eat an 'oyster loaf'; oysters left to bake very slowly in a buttered brown bread loaf. My mother told me that, if you sat on the sofa in the front parlour, you could prop your feet up on the opposite wall. I was a very quiet baby – my cot was just behind the thin wall that backed the big grand piano – and I would sleep undisturbed through all the music-making night after night.

I remember my mother's father. He called me 'Jimmy' – they had all so hoped that I would be a boy. He always sat in a green corduroy armchair in the sunshine – the kind that had twisting knobs, to make it low or high or reclining, which of course was fascinating. He also had a white walrus moustache and a lovely warm clean smell and a heavy gold watch chain, with a still heavier watch in his waistcoat pocket.

Mother had two sisters and two brothers. Matilda who had the singing voice and who became a Christian Science Practitioner; Ernestine who was very fat and lazy and disappeared into the Middle West; Sidney, with a glossy moustache, who travelled a lot and brought me huge 'unplayworthy' dolls from all over the world, and Louis who looked like Napoleon and had hay fever. There had been a third brother, Alex, who had died of yellow fever when he was twelve. They were all musical, impractical and loved life. My grandfather, presiding over his family at dinner, once said: 'Anything you want – just ask for it – and you won't get it!' He thought that was very funny.

Father's was a different background – a very large continental family. I am told now by my one remaining cousin in France that an early ancestor came from Spain. The story goes that, in the Franco-Prussian War, a later ancestor was living on the Prussian border of what was then Alsace-Lorraine. When the German army came, he quickly changed his name to Elsas (Alsace), thus escaping complications, and Elsas remained the family name. It was at the end of the First World War, when I had been offered a contract with the Metropolitan Opera

House in New York, that the management insisted that I change my name to Ellis, because Elsas sounded German. I am sorry about that now. One wants to be who one *is*.

*   *   *

The first trip to Europe that I remember was when I was four years old, at the end of May. We left in a hired horse-drawn bus – seating eight, four to a side – to drive through New York to the docks. The ship was one of the old German-American liners. I was sick with excitement before I got to it. I shared a cabin with my sister and Alice, my sister looking pea-green, her red-gold plaits swinging over the side of an upper berth, moaning 'I want to die'.

I woke up on my fifth birthday, June 15th 1905, at a hotel in London; on a red-plush chair by my bed were presents – the only one I kept was a little golden locket in the shape of a heart. My favourite pastime was not the usual one of toys and dolls: it was the yellow manila scribble paper from father's mills. Big sheets of it on the floor, crayons and pencils, and a whole afternoon would pass happily.

In Paris, that fifth year of being alive, I was taken to the Louvre and am told that I walked up and down between the great Greek statues, gazing at them intently. When I came back to the hotel, I proceeded to draw a figure with a very large penis, Greek or otherwise. With pride I asked 'Is that a man?' To my mother's credit she kept a straight face and said 'Yes dear' – so I was spared curiosity and inhibitions for ever.

Then we went to a spa – I think it was Marienbad – for my mother's indigestion. Alice took me every afternoon to where nurses, mothers and children gathered – a stall in the park, where a very clean brown and white cow was milked into small mugs and the children drank the warm foaming liquid, smelling slightly of stables. I hated it all. Alice reported that I had refused this elixir, whereupon I got the first and only spanking my mother ever gave me, with the back of a hair-

1 My father, Herman Elsas

3 With my sister, Lucile in 1901

2 My mother, Caroline Reinhardt Elsas

4 Myself aged two-and-a-half

5 My first operatic role, a school
production of *Hansel and Gretel*, 1909

6 & 7 Myself and Lucile on the voyage
back to New York in 1910

brush on my bottom. So in fear I drank the milk the next day, and was very sick for a week afterwards. I have never liked milk since, and the sight of a cow's swinging, damp udder fills me with revulsion. Let psychiatrists make of that what they will. But I had to milk cows in World War II.

During those early years we spent several months in rented houses on the New Jersey coast. The grey, wild Atlantic frightened me. Even on fine days the waves were huge and relentless, whipped into white foam and spray. I had a white flannel bathing suit with never seemed to dry and my father had a dark blue one which came to his knees. He would take me on his back and swim, and I would cling to him and feel safe. One day he purposely let me go thinking, I suppose, that I would swim instinctively, but I didn't, and was hauled out, filled with sea-water and a mighty dread of the waves, and with the trust in my father sadly diminished. I tried year after year to learn to swim and never managed it until my sixty-fourth birthday, when a wise friend suggested that I should try the breast-stroke while singing a waltz; this I did, to the amazement of the sun-bathing French, surprised out of their oiled apathy on a beach near St Tropez.

One day I let the canary out of its cage. The memory of my father cavorting all over the garden, trying to recapture the poor bird under a wicker waste-paper basket, still haunts me. I didn't get scolded about the canary, but what I *did* get scolded for was the wilting hydrangea. It grew in a large tub, filled with lovely peaty earth. Week after week the plant had to be renewed. Mother finally found out that I used the tub every afternoon for a purpose for which it was never intended; the days seemed full of unreasonable punishments.

Alice took me to a famous sweet shop where, if I had been good all week, I was allowed to have an ice-cream. There were little white iron tables and chairs, and the waitress would bring two telephone books to put on my chair so that I could reach the mountain of ice-cream easily. One day, after we had finished, we walked back along the sea road. And then it happened. A beautiful pair of black horses drawing a Victoria, with two ladies out for their afternoon drive, came smartly down the lane. From a hidden drive-way one of the new monsters, a red motor-car, hurtled onto the road – the horses reared, but did not stop, and the car cut into the horses, overturning the carriage. There were screams, whinnies, spurting blood, and I remember Alice seizing me and covering my eyes and then running, running with me till we reached home. For days afterwards there were whispers of the tragedy and for nights afterwards nightmares, until our doctor gave me some sticky syrup that made me sleep.

Those very early years were punctuated by diptheria and whooping cough. These mysteries upset me and I was allowed out of bed too soon after diptheria, developing a limp, which worried my parents a lot, until a doctor in Bavaria told Mother that it was only fallen arches and I was put into great hunky shoes until I learned to walk properly again.

After all that, it was wonderful to roller-skate in the Mall on winter afternoons in Central Park. And if Alice thought I deserved it, I was allowed to buy rides in the little goat-drawn wagons which went up and down the Mall for a dime a time. I had a terrible sailor-hat, made of stiff patent-leather with a tight elastic under my chin, which I hated, and a Tartan dress which I loathed, and a little boyfriend who tried to make me blink with an open penknife jabbing at my face. He accidentally pierced my cheek and I have the scar still. Otherwise I'm sure I was happy.

One day, when I was playing under the trees near the reservoir (the bridle path went all round it) the cry of 'Runaway horse, look out!' startled everybody; Alice turned over a park bench and put another little girl and me under it. Soon, a wild-looking bay came careering along with a young girl in a black riding habit, side-saddle, clinging to the horse's mane, her red-gold hair streaming out behind her, a policeman on horseback in full pursuit. 'It's my sister,' I screamed. Indeed it was.

The year when I was seven we were in Switzerland and Bavaria and I was sometimes sent with my sister on her walks with various young gentlemen who sought her company. I remember especially a Greek, who went up to Oxford and had a strange dark mother who lived in Alexandria. I was plumped down in a corn field to wait for them while they took a walk. I remember, too, a Russian who thought my very Western sister, with her gorgeous red hair, was just the girl to grace a St Petersburg household in those pre-revolution days; and a young man of the Hungarian Esterhazy family. She eventually went back to New York and married Horace Liveright, who became a publisher and who made her miserable for a great part of her life. I am told that I burst into tears when she became engaged to him. I was much more in favour of her other suitor, Walter Lippmann, who became that most distinguished political author and was always on time when he called. As my sister was always late, I was sent downstairs to talk to him while he waited for her. I remember his interest and kindness to a little girl. A big, gentle, pale young man, I know he wanted to marry her.

I wish now so much that I could remember all about her – but she was growing up then and to her I was an infant. Even in Paris, I cannot remember her. The Champs Elysées Punch and Judy shows in the afternoon were my delight – and the hot chocolate – and of course the visits to the Louvre and the wide, gravel walks in the Tuileries, where funny little French boys, always very pale, with thin knees, large dark eyes and slightly smelly, played hide and seek behind the statues and urns.

Alice was dismissed in favour of a governess that winter of 1907. I can remember her crying as my mother, sitting at the desk, told her I must keep on speaking French and German and that a governess had been engaged. It was the end of the world for me. A great dark grief that only an unreasoning child can feel. I was betrayed and alone.

*   *   *

The governess' name was Irma Freund. I wonder why the memory of governesses so often spells doom-watch? Perhaps the puzzled transition from infancy to disciplined childhood remains a sad ache, and the blame must be put somewhere.

Unrealised by my parents – I was too scared to complain or to tell them about it – the reign of Irma Freund was for a me a short-lived hell, full of treachery and of learning all the wrong things, and I was frightened out of my wits. I would pretend to be asleep in order to watch her prepare for the night. She had beautiful teeth, so I waited in vain for her to deposit them in a glass of water, as Alice had done. Instead, I watched her remove a long thick tail of hair that was brushed and put away in her top drawer until morning. Before breakfast she was always very cross. A hard hair-brush was banged on my head when I fidgeted. Instead of a walk in the afternoon, I was taken to a house in the Bronx where some very large and serious Germans sat around a table endlessly talking of the Vaterland and drinking coffee and beer. I was told to sit on the floor and play with some building blocks, which I felt was insulting to my years. The strange atmosphere – secret and harsh – impressed itself on me; now, if I see films about German concentration camps, I am reminded of Fräulein Freund. She was finally dismissed because she had taken me to spend hours at a tuberculosis exhibition at the Natural History Museum. This was full of explicit photographs and diagrams and ghastly wax models of lungs and other inner organs, which made me feel sick. I never had another governess – only school.

The house was always full of visiting musicians who seemed to have no interest in anything except food. The morning-glory horn of the gramophone droned out symphonies, slightly scratchy, and Nellie Melba sounding like a distant train whistle, Adelina Patti fluting Tosti's 'Goodbye', Preludes from Wagnerian operas, and sometimes, to my delight, Viennese waltzes.

Before Alice left, I had had my first visit to the theatre; it was some kind of indoor circus at the big Hippodrome in New York, with a great clown, Marceline – baggy trousers and a sad, sad face. His act was to keep on trying to do something and always being too late, or failing, or falling over his oversize shoes. For some reason we were in a box at the side of the stage; Alice was in charge. Someone on the stage asked 'What time is it?' and Marcelline took a huge watch out of his pocket and said 'Three o'clock', whereupon, to the great amusement of the audience, I said in a very loud voice 'Time for my cocoa, Allie!' Perhaps that was the spark that fired me to want an audience. I remember the startled, friendly look from round painted eyes as Marceline stopped his run across the stage and waved to me.

I can't remember much about school. When I came home at one o'clock there would be lunch in a dark dining-room and then Mother would make me practise the piano. But all I cared about was drawing. Of course, I fell in love with my English teacher at school, who had the unforgettable name of Susan Sayre Titsworth and smelled of lavender. She wore heliotrope tweed and a circlet of stringy grey braids about her head – a dim, sad woman who encouraged me to read everything and to write – even to the point of writing plays and poems – the first poem being a very socially-conscious effort for a ten year old:

> The evening sky is like a beggar's coat
> Not like a prince's raiment, jewelled and fine,
> In many places it is ragged and torn
> Through which the light of glory seems to shine.

(very embarrassing now)

Miss Titsworth coached me much later to pass examinations which might have taken me to college, if my life had not been geared to music and theatre. During these years too, I was taken to see Charles Dana Gibson, of Gibson Girl fame, to get his advice about art study. He sent me to the 57th Street Art Students' League where I copied Antique sculpture in charcoal, and later went into a life-class, which shocked me. I pretended to be older than I was and apart from feeling sick at my first sight of an ugly nude gentleman model, so unlike the Greek statues in the Louvre, I managed to learn a lot.

In the summer of 1911, in Bad Kissingen, Bavaria, while my mother was taking a cure at Dr Dapper's Clinic I was taken care of by my Tante Emma at the Hotel Viktoria. She was a bird-like, pretty little woman – my uncle's widow. What fascinated me was how she could eat a pigeon so that only a tiny heap of bones remained on her plate. A sort of mini-cannibalism.

Her husband, my father's brother Siegmund, had been a cosy, bearded man who sang Lieder very seriously, but what had impressed me most when I was taken to visit her was a wonderful pudding for dessert – a very sweet meringue four inches high, laced through with ripe red-currants that popped juicily in one's mouth – 'Preusselbeerenkuchen' – what a name for ambrosia! At the Viktoria Hotel, too, a Russian family stayed every year. They had two little girls and we played in that Proustian garden. I can see white starched dresses, dappled with sunshine, and hear voices saying 'catch me Maria', dissolving into laughter.

I shared a room with my sister and I would wake up often to find her sitting up in bed, one lamp on, writing her endless love-letters to Horace Liveright, her sheaf of red hair falling over her shoulders and face. I would pretend to be asleep and feel like a conspirator because I knew my parents were hoping that her sojourn in Europe would make her forget all about him. It didn't, of course.

Music played at the Kursaal at 7.30 in the morning while quiet ladies and gentlemen seemed to glide among the trees drinking mugs of sulphur-water through glass tubes. I was allowed to go and walk among them and listen to the music, and got as near the bandstand as I could. Sometimes I would meet my mother on her early walk to a café where she would have a second breakfast. One of the patients in the Clinic was William Gillette, the American actor who had made Sherlock Holmes his own. He adored my mother and did his best to win me over. He would take me for long walks in the poppy-studded corn-fields and tell me marvellous stories. On my birthday – that June – a huge box came from him, tied with pink ribbon. I was terribly excited and opened it – inside it was a smaller one – and then another – and so on, until I came to one about three inches square, tied again with ribbons; inside was a card; 'Your birthday cake, but don't eat it!' I opened it to find a doll's size cake of soap. I still think it was a horrid thing to do – and I hated him, and all the grown-ups who laughed.

I suppose that these early summers were the happiest times of my life. My father would meet us in the Engadin, with its sun-lit valleys and snow-capped Alps, deep blue lakes and air like wine. He would take me on walks early in the morning, ending up for breakfast at some Konditorei, perhaps to Hanselman's in St Moritz; the long talks with him setting a pattern for my future behaviour.

I realise now what a true romantic he was; he carried a small morocco-bound edition of his favourite book, Cervantes' *Don Quixote*, in his pocket. He taught me that I would have to work hard for anything I wanted in life – but made me feel that he would always be on my side. I wish so much now that I had known him better; it was my mother's faintly cynical realistic attitude that always brought us down a peg. I came home from an Alpine walk one day and said I had seen someone looking like the Archangel Gabriel striding down the mountainside, the sun shining through an aureole of blonde hair, his loden-cape flying out behind him like wings. 'That's the young conductor Leopold Stokowski' my father said. 'His name is Stokes' said my mother and the conversation ended there. Father took me to see the new Stuttgart Opera Houses, built like two Greek Temples on a lake in the Park. The bigger House was for the dramatic operas, the smaller one for the lighter works of Mozart, Offenbach and others. They were joined by a colonnade at the lake-side. It seemed to me that nothing lovelier could happen than to come out onto the balustraded roof between the Acts, into the moonlight, and watch the swans glide on the inky blue lake. We went back-stage to see all the latest stage mechanisms and the artists' dressing-rooms and I was filled with a new curiosity about this world of work and fantasy, singing as it went along. But a frightening thing was the room where all the wigs were made. It affected me then in the way 'The Muppet Show' sometimes affects me now.

Back to the Alpine meadows. They were full of gentians and sweet smelling daphne, caramel coloured cows, and music-box chalets. No cars were allowed there then and we travelled either on those miraculous railways – through tunnels up and up, watching the same village re-appear as the train wound higher and higher – or in an open carriage with four horses, brakes full on, down hill over mountain-passes all the way to Italy. I was allowed to sit in the high seat next to the coachman and went through alternate moments of ecstasy and fright, totally overawed by the sight of a glacier lying like a heart-shaped emerald between high peaks, and delighted by the little lizards that darted about as they scuttled for crumbs and grapes at the journey's end in Chiavenna.

I think of a child's face pressed hard against the glass of a train window; warm hands outspread making finger marks, the train chuffing into distances unknown.

*   *   *

It was always exciting, to come back to New York in a big ship every autumn. On one voyage in 1910 all the stars of the Metropolitan Opera House were returning for rehearsals. Thinking of that group of ego-maniacs now, it is amazing to remember how beautiful they then seemed to me; those large gentlemen in fur-collared coats humming garlic-wise and musically, as they marched around the deck; sounds of laughter and gutteral languages. But above all I remember Geraldine Farrar smiling at me as she passed by, wrapped in chinchilla, with gardenias and orchids and leaving a trail of perfume. After that I was completely stage-struck. More than a decade later I made my début at the Metropolitan in the première of the Puccini tryptich, with her as Suor Angelica and me as Suor Genovieffa. Of course she did not recognise me.

That winter I was taken to my first opera. I cannot remember my downfall, so how can I describe it? Except that I sat enchanted, despite my first long gloves and too-tight patent leather shoes. My mother strove in vain to impress upon me that opera was a mish-mash of the arts – to me it was magic. My untrained voice yowled through the wet winter afternoons. The enthusiasm was finally controlled when the school put on *Hansel and Gretel* and there were rehearsals and direction. I was delirious with joy and loved every minute of playing and singing Gretel. Nothing ever again gave me quite the same uncomplicated thrill.

Of course I knew absolutely nothing about anything. I just decided I wanted to be an opera-singer and that was that. The painting and drawing went on, as did school lessons, but everything stopped each summer when my father took the family to Europe, on a mixture of business and family visits.

One of Mother's friends was Maude Meyer, who lived in London. Originally from a Polish family, she had married an Englishman and had two sons. She somehow knew I was hungry for direction and discipline and she also knew my mother's feckless approach to such matters, so she undertook the thankless task of making me conscious of the technical-ities, the work, the academic approach to music. I am grateful to her now but then I was almost resentful and only enjoyed it when she took me to the opera. She expected, and constantly demanded, admiration and, even though I was fascinated, like a small rabbit, by her seeming understanding, I felt a certain discomfort.

Her younger son played the violin and later wrote twenty books under the name of Hugh Merrick, took magnificent photographs and was more knowledgeable about music and mountains than anyone I ever knew. He also managed to have a perfect marriage, which I think was his greatest achievement. And he remained my friend over seventy-odd years.

Mother and I went to Munich that summer of 1912 for a few weeks; I cannot remember why. We stayed in a pension; it was a pleasant house, full of medical and music students. It stood opposite the Lenbach Museum, where the famous German portrait-painter had lived and worked. His lovely sepia drawings were very popular then, but what intrigued me most was the fountain in his garden, where water gushed out of the nipples of full-breasted stone nymphs – very Germanic. And we went for coffee or tea every afternoon to the Künstler-Haus where students gathered and where I could gaze at a very ugly boy who I thought looked like Beethoven, who was my god of the moment. My mother seemed to identify herself with all my youthful emotions – as though she had missed them herself – but in the end this proved very bad for me as she condoned much too much, without understand-ing enough, and I had to find out everything the hard way. I got no answers to the usual adolescent questions; by the time I was grown-up I felt much older than she was.

We saw a wonderful Reinhardt production of *The Mikado* and the visits to the museums, to the opera and walks and drives in fiacres have left me with many memories, but I have

never been back to Munich – or to Germany for that matter –
since those days before World War I.

During those holidays too, I had fallen in love. It is absurd
to think that a precocious girl of twelve cannot love deeply.
Rupert came from Manchester and our families had been
meeting for several years on the alpine holidays. His mother
was a worldly-wise woman whose turquoise and diamond
jewellery and grey chiffon evening dresses seemed very
romantic to me. Everyone called her 'Lieschen', even her sons.
Rupert was a tall, grey-eyed boy of seventeen when we first
met and through subsequent summers we became great
friends. He was at Clare College, Cambridge, studying to be a
surgeon. I was madly hurt and jealous when he took an older
girl friend to tea and when, during May-week at Cambridge,
he was host to a sophisticated girl called Poppy!

But suddenly everything changed. I got great comfort out
of holding his warm Meerschaum pipe; he smiled at this
always – perhaps he was already aware of such Freudian
manifestations, even if I wasn't – but when he asked to kiss me
I said I would have to ask my mother, which I did and she said
'You must decide that for yourself'. So I went back to him and
told him he could kiss my cheek. He laughed and took my two
long braids and tied them under my chin and made me
promise never to cut them off. I can see his face clearly
whenever I want to – it would not take more than a breath
between then and now to hear his young and comforting
voice making some idiotic, and oh so English pun.

There were only two years more before World War I. I was
studying like mad, pushed on by my ever-zealous mother, so I
rebelled and left home for three months in the summer and
went to Chateaugay Lake on the border of Canada, where one
of my teachers, Alys Bentley, had a school. She was a remarkable woman with a noble Roman face and a short mane of
grey hair; she had taught music and choral singing for years
and had developed an amazing combination of yoga, euryth-

mics, dancing exercises, vegetarianism, and relaxation. Her pupils all learned to cook and eat in a way that has become commonplace today. She called it all 'fundamentalism'. Children were taught music through movement. I became a demonstration pupil – and enjoyed it, even if constantly sitting on damp grass gave me life-long twinges of sciatica.

I slept in a cubicle in the hay-loft with a broom by my bed because the bats scared me, whirring past my nose in the dark. One night there was a fancy-dress party and a very thin girl, who had painted large patches of brown on her naked self and said she was 'the afternoon of a faun', climbed up to my room in the barn, expecting I knew not what – and went away quickly when I said I'd tell Miss Bentley in the morning. Ignorance or innocence protected me at the oddest moments. I was very puzzled.

Then back to New York and more lessons. That May we sailed for the Continent as usual – there was London and a visit to Manchester to spend a weekend with Rupert's family. Then Switzerland again and a goodbye to him in a Zürich garden. Recently, I went back there to try to recapture its secret if I could, but it is ridiculous to do these things.

At the end of July 1914, we went back to Paris again. It was very hot; the air buzzed with rumours and fears. I remember feeling apprehensive and miserable and yet violently excited about nothing in particular. And then it came suddenly, the fear-bubble burst, and my mother and I were hustled out of Paris with other aliens, as the gatling-guns on the roofs rattled into the night sky. We were pushed into a crowded cattle-truck bound for Marseilles and ordered to get back to the United States as best we could, and as quickly as possible. World War I had begun.

Marseilles was thronged with every kind of uniform. The Zouaves cheered and grinned and paraded in lines along the boulevards, Chinese boys sold drugs and windmills and fans and poisonous-looking sweets; prostitutes giggled and locked arms with the soldiers, their bosoms tight in satin, great crescent moons of sweat under their arms. The streets smelled terrible; the hotel we were sent to was awful and there was no ship sailing for at least ten days. My poor mother must have been very miserable – but I was over the moon with excitement. Even sleeping in a bed with my mother, on a mattress seemingly filled with a haystack, and having a perpetual stomach-ache, didn't dim my enthusiasm.

About the third day, a young man introduced himself. He, too, was a refugee from Paris, waiting for a ship. Lee Simonson was an artist who had been working and living in Paris. He offered his services as escort for the days of waiting and proved to be a good companion. We went on picnics to Cassis and swam in a hot sea while Mother, with her black sun-shade open, sat on a chair on the beach, watching. Lee took my operatic dreams seriously and gave me my first feeling of self-confidence; besides this he started my interest in French painting, particularly the Impressionists, and modern French music; but all this came later, after we had reached New York.

The *Patria* was a tub of a ship. It should have carried one hundred-and-fifty passengers, but four hundred were packed into it – four or six to a cabin. We stopped in Spain – Almeria, hot and dusty, its beggars sitting on the Cathedral steps like dismembered crows. Then on to the Azore Islands – Pont Delgada, where hydrangeas grew wild, and bluer than the sky and sea; moss was knee-deep. The women were all in black, faceless in deep hoods, while the men sported every bright colour. From this remote paradise we embarked on a stormy sea-voyage that took three weeks. We lived on grapes, ripe olives, biscuits and what my mother called 'condemned army-horses'. She allowed me to wind my two plaits of hair around my head – but I don't think she realised how quickly I had grown up under Lee Simonson's tutelage.

We reached New York on an Indian Summer day in September 1914. My father was at the dock, relieved to see us

safely returned from what New Yorkers called the 'war-
zone'. I had almost forgotten all about it on that journey, but
now it all rushed back. Rupert going to France as a dispatch-
rider with the army, twenty-one years old; the goodbye in the
Zürich garden, the last frightening day in Paris and that
crowded cattle-truck on the train to Marseilles filled with
women and children. All this receded day by day; the clarion-
call of clear October days in New York, the new routine of
work, the burning ambition that gobbled up lessons and
teachers, and friends. I must have been the most awful teen-
ager, as violent in my own way as the ones that rampage and
rebel in any age. It was just good luck that the energy and
egocentricity was channelled into a passion for achievement
and that my parents were so understanding.

*   *   *

I heard low-voiced and serious talk between my parents about
the likelihood of war, but was too engrossed in endless lessons
to listen to anyone but my teachers. I received rather battered
looking regulation postcards marked 'British Expeditionary
Force' from France – just saying 'I am well and send love'
from Rupert – and an occasional longer letter with sentences
completely blacked out by the censor. But even these reminders became more and more unreal. Now I am shocked to
think how unaware the young people were of what was going
on in the world – so unlike those of today.

My singing teacher was Mrs Ashforth, a Belgian contralto
who had married an Englishman. Her name had been Frieda
de Goebele and she had taught many famous singers. She was
a remarkable old lady of eighty when I started to work with
her. Every morning at nine o'clock I was in her house for two
hours. She would come down to her salon, after suffering a
sleepless night of chronic asthma, always dressed in bright
colours, jewels on her fingers and in her ears, white hair piled
high. She would sit at her piano, which she played atrociously,

and explain in a word what she wanted. I can remember all her vocalises; those printed scales and phrases to practise every day, composed by a gentleman called 'Panofka'. 'Sing across the sea to France' – she would say – or 'Put a tea-cup over that note' or 'That scale sounds like bad knitting'. There was no question of 'little' thinking with her. She made me start studying all the opera scores immediately – whether they suited my voice or not. Fortunately I spoke French and German, so only the Italian was new to me. Some weeks were devoted entirely to songs – Arie Antiche, French Bergerettes, little-known German songs of Franz and Reichhardt. These would seem the easier weeks. But later I realized that the singing of songs needs more intensive study than the huge canvas of a dramatic opera.

Sometimes Mrs Ashforth asked an established singer to attend the lessons. These were frightening mornings followed by hours of corrections and admonitions. Sometimes I would arrive at her house and wait for an hour and then I would know she was recovering from one of her awful bronchial attacks. Eventually she would appear on the arm of her companion housekeeper – a tall, thin woman, always dressed in black, like a Victorian villainess.

I had kept up lessons with Alys Bentley. They supplied, I suppose, the necessary physical exercise which would otherwise have been lacking. She had a ringing voice which could raise the roof, and a kind of robust earthiness, the complete opposite to Mrs Ashforth who, more than anyone I ever knew, was what the French call 'une femme racée'. But it was Miss Bentley who helped me over many of the stumbling-blocks of extreme shyness which has always been an agony for me. As long as there was a character to hide behind – and the footlights between me and 'them' – it was all right. I could never perform happily at concerts, or 'charity do's', or even at rehearsals, or look forward to a big party and this shyness remains with me even now.

Somewhere during these years I saw both Sarah Bernhardt and Eleanora Duse on their last tours. Bernhardt was performing excerpts from her famous plays; *Camille, Phèdre* and a terrible one-acter about a soldier in the trenches. She must have had her wooden leg already, I think, as she sat down for all her scenes. I can hear her voice, so golden-strangled, saying 'Mon fils – mon fils' in *Phèdre* – and her dying words in *Camille*. I can see, too, her white face with its lowering cloud of dry red fuzzy hair, her bad teeth and her large middle with its belted low waist-line. Even so, she was magical.

But later, when I saw the great Duse, it was more wonderful. No make-up, playing a girl of seventeen, even if her hair was almost white, you believed everything she did and said . . . and I saw her playing Mrs Alving in *Ghosts*; with her back to the audience, her shoulder-blades under the black alpaca dress tense and tortured. I bought violets and stood in the lobby of the Hotel Majestic in New York, waiting for her to return from the theatre. Some words of thanks from that frail quiet woman and I walked in a dream. A few weeks later she was dead in a smoky American city, Pittsburgh – unmourned by an uncaring audience – and deserted by her great lover, d'Annunzio. In the cast of her plays was a slim young actor, Tullio Carminati; in Hollywood twenty years later I was filming *Paris Love Song* with Tullio and one of my loveliest possessions is a Georgian silver ink-well inscribed in rather Italianate wording 'Only happy hours Mary dear. March 1935'. He told me a lot about his youthful experiences working with Duse and was the only non-egomaniacal male film-star I ever met. But that's years ahead of my story.

I saw Pavlova dance only once – it was certain enchantment; I even followed her one day as she was going into one of New York's big department stores. She was dressed strangely – rather like some aunt who lives in Menton and visits the family very seldom, lots of chiffon veiling and a floppy hat; her small white face almost disappearing – shopping and talking in halting English.

8 'Harper's Bazaar', 1925

9 Antonio Scotti

To
Mary Ellis
with best wishes
A Scotti
New York
Dec 1921

10 Geraldine Farrar as Carmen at the
Metropolitan Opera, New York

I also followed the boxer, Carpentier, one morning, all the way down Fifth Avenue. When I came home and told my mother these things she was not amused, and I was told it was rude and ridiculous. I wonder what she'd say to the fans of today who wait and yell and demand attention? I'd have had my answer ready because one of her favourite stories was how she tore the rose from her bosom and threw it onto the platform where it fell at Paderewski's feet after a concert. I think it is only that the gesture has changed. Then fans gave something to their idols; today they demand things of them. They practically tear them apart and, if they don't like their efforts to entertain them, there is hell to pay. Perhaps it is all because films and theatre have become so much more accessible; there is no longer a pedestalled world of skilled showmanship and wonder, like the elephant on a turning globe; it is a free-for-all fight.

These were the years when most girls would have begun to go to parties, and meet boys, and have school-girlish 'best friends'. Instead, besides practising and lessons, I was sent to a Russian dance-master and was physically tortured for a few months, until he gave up in despair. I only got as far as work at the barre, purple in the face and aching in every muscle. (I repeated that physical agony a quarter of a century later when I learned to ski, but that had its compensations!) These were the years of highbrow adolescence. My friends were budding musicians and poets; one Leo Ornstein – a hideous but talented young pianist; another Edwin Justus Mayer who years later wrote a splendid play, *Children of Darkness*, for me, but was then thin and very Jewish and prone to tears. My mother's remark one day: 'Why can't you know anyone who can give you more than a book?' made a lasting impression, but I never have been able to think in such terms.

I remember sitting on the floor in Lee Simonson's Greenwich Village studio; going through the phase of Russian literature, Baudelaire's *Fleurs du Mal*, modern French painting; meeting all the budding young directors of what became the famous Theatre Guild, who were starting then as a group to put on very special plays in a stable-turned-theatre, very 'fringe', also in the Village; and lunching in an artists' café, John Reed at the head of the long table, with young writers and painters hanging on his every word.

Looking back, I can understand completely the present day maturity of fifteen-year-olds – there's nothing unusual about it – we were the same, but more self-conscious and not as sex-conscious. Innocence is an ingrown thing; it is a human quality that can dominate the character and persist despite all kinds of experiences. It has nothing to do with what one *knows*.

Parallel with all this was a rigorous discipline, and my mother's ambition for me to succeed. Every Sunday there were concerts; during the week at least one opera; and even if I got to bed late, the lessons started at nine o'clock. My hero-worship was still for Geraldine Farrar, the leading opera singer at the Metropolitan. From my childhood onwards there had been a correspondence; hundreds of letters from the day I met her in Germany before World War I, until she died in the 1960s. After she left the opera I saw her very seldom – but always at crucial times in my life – and I visited her for the last time in the late fifties in her little house in Ridgefield, Connecticut. The old glamour of chiffon and pink roses, chinchilla and perfume had gone; she was very much a blue-rinsed, stout, political-minded lady, violently Republican, but the eyes still reflected the sky and her smile still struck deep. She refused to talk about her operatic past – saying: 'That was another world'. The only obvious reminder of her opera days was a large portrait of Toscanini dominating the walls of her bungalow.

In the summer of 1916, my parents took a small house in New Jersey because the Italian operatic coach, Fernando Tanara, was teaching there. He had six pupils who shared his time. A gentle tyrant, a little man with a big soft beard, a rose-bud mouth and a virago of a wife who organised his pupils. I have never understood the word 'coach'. Is it because the person drives you along a road and gets you somewhere? Tanara certainly did that. I found myself having to learn every word and note of Italian and French operas so thoroughly that even now I feel I could re-learn them all with only a few days' study. He had tenors, baritones, mezzos and contraltos all to hand, so that one sang with other singers. We ate, slept, lived and breathed opera – in fact so much so, that I lost all perspective of real living, to be rudely awakened occasionally.

A German conductor, Bodanzky, also had a house near-by and he came in and out of our music-room all summer. He looked like a balding raven and I was scared of him and his continual insinuations, but my mother encouraged his visits. I suspect she thought he could, or would, help me in some way. This embarrassed and worried me.

And so that hot, mosquito-bitten summer (nowhere are there such big mosquitoes as in New Jersey) wore on. When the day's study was over I would sit down and write to Rupert, still on active service in France, and his vague printed war-cards kept arriving. People kept saying 'The war will end soon'; but it seemed a life-time since my mother and I had had that voyage home on the S.S. *Patria*.

One hot day in early July, Mother took the train into New York, and in the afternoon I went to the station to meet her on her return. As she stepped off the train I noticed that she was pale and very silent. My first thought was that she had gone into town to see a doctor, and that she was ill, but when I asked her she said 'Wait until we get home'. When we got to the house we went up to my room and she told me she had been to New York to verify the news that Rupert had been killed. He had died of the shock of having his leg amputated after being severely wounded that first of July in the Battle of the Somme.

Everything I had been doing for the past two years seemed suddenly ridiculous; I can only remember lying on my bed

that day and my father coming in towards evening to put on a
lamp and making me drink something. There is a great hole in
my memory here; when I could focus again, I found I had cut
off my hair; Rupert alive had made me promise never to do so.
I suppose it was my statement of dedication to him, a youthful
gesture of defiance in the face of my first encounter with death
and love. Of course I got over it; life began again, lessons
began again, the future began again.

*   *   *

The days shortened into another winter. But I had to make
new reasons for achievement since Rupert was not there to
watch it happen. My mother's encouragement was obsessive,
though I was startled now and then by her odd ways of
reasoning. I said to her one day that I was shocked to hear that
a singer we knew was 'living in sin' with someone. Her
answer was: 'She can do anything – she is a great artist'. At
that age my moral sense was too fanatical to consider her
viewpoint seriously.

   That winter I worked harder than ever. My room was a
sunny bed-sitter, with an upright piano and a big desk; I was
allowed to have my friends up there. The house was one of
those tall, narrow ones that were lined up like an army over
the streets of New York before sky-scraper apartment-houses
took over. The broad tram-lined avenues, and elevated rail-
roads over shopping streets, were safe for everyone; I walked
all over the city and can only remember being frightened
twice – once by an ambling drunk, and another day in the
pouring rain, when a very wet gentleman stood in my path
exposing himself. When I told my mother, she was more
curious and amused than shocked, and asked for details. I
never understood her lack of worldliness. Never once, even in
the emotional crises of my life, when I needed her help, did she
ever explain anything to me. I'm convinced it was because she
didn't know.

The next summer, 1917, we followed Tanara again, this time to a country town in upper New York State. My other teacher, Mrs Ashforth, came to visit us in our rented house and father came every weekend. The great excitement was my first public concert – Tanara's pupils at the Town Hall. I sang a Mozart duet with the baritone; also one from Massenet's *Thaïs* and 'Who is Sylvia?' Later that week the baritone took me for a buggy ride in the country. Behind a steaming brown mare I sat on a very uncomfortable leather seat, with the swarthy young Armenian holding the reins – it was horrid. He looked like one of Ali Baba's forty thieves. Years later my mother told me he had come back to see her one day and, after reminding her who he was, sold her two Persian prayer-rugs.

Lee Simonson came up for this historic concert. I had made myself a white dress with silver flowers woven into it – very eighteenth century – because I was singing Mozart, of course. I cannot remember a single thing about that evening except that I stayed up very late after it, in front of an open fire, talking to Lee, and drinking cocoa, and hearing a declaration of love from him – which thrilled me much more than the concert had. Tanara was very pleased and in a month's time we were all back in New York, with the United States on the verge of going into the war and New York playing at austerity.

Sons of my family's friends were going off to France; there were parades of departing soldiers on Fifth Avenue – anti-Kaiser posters, Red Cross training, Ivor Novello's 'Keep The Home Fires Burning', 'And We Won't Come Back Till It's Over, Over There' sung rousingly by Nora Bayes.

The winter was very cold. Tanara wanted me to have an audition in the spring. He said if the war had not happened I would have been going to Italy to get my training in some little opera house, before trying for the big ones – in Milan or Naples. So he wanted me, instead, to sing for the directors of the Metropolitan Opera House 'just to get their advice and find out what we are to do with you'. He chose a scene from Massenet's *Manon* and I spent hours acting it out in my room and more hours rehearsing it in Tanara's studio. The only person who knew about the audition, apart from my parents, was Miss Bentley, who promised to find her way somehow to a seat in the dark 'Diamond Horseshoe' of the Opera House and to wave her handkerchief if all had gone well.

Three days before the audition I developed laryngitis. Drastic measures were applied and after inhaling Friar's Balsam, leaning on my hand for half an hour, I lifted my head to find my jaw was dislocated. The doctor came, gave me a whiff of chloroform, strapped the jaw up with adhesive tape, and said: 'I *hope* it will set – I can't promise.' My father squeezed lemons and oranges which I drank through a glass tube – only forty-eight hours to the audition. I was in tears, in despair – in a rage.

The next day the tapes were taken off, the jaw was in place, and I started practising. My heart pounded into my throat; my stomach turned over incessantly; my knees were jelly. Two days later I walked out onto the huge stage of the Metropolitan Opera House. I was very small and it was vast and dark; one working light threw great shadows across the stage. Halfway back in the stalls sat five huddled figures, the directors. A feeling of doom. Tanara went before me to the piano, with the score of *Manon*. I followed him on, and with an arrogant assurance I have never found since, asked for a table and chair in order to do my scene. A very surprised voice from the stalls ordered a stage-hand to bring them – and a more surprised stage-hand placed a scruffy table and chair in the middle of the stage. Tanara played the first bit quietly; music and the table became candle-lit; on it were two glasses half filled with wine. Was it nerves, or the misery of that French girl alone in eighteenth-century Paris? 'Adieu, notre petite table.' A dead silence. I had sung the scene – I had acted like *mad*. What would Gatti-Casazza say? Would he tell me to give up the idea of an operatic career, or what? I sat down on the spindly chair in the middle of that bare stage and waited, shaking, suddenly frozen. Tanara went down into the stalls to speak to the four vultures. I looked up towards the tiers of boxes and saw a white handkerchief waving in the blackness. So Miss Bentley had managed to get in, after all. I came to, a bit, then. Suddenly I saw Tanara coming towards me: 'Cara, Cara,' he cried, and he *was* crying, but smiling too. 'They want you *here*, next season, and for three seasons after that – *now* you will really have to work!'

The contract would start at $150 a week, rising $100 each season. I was to prepare all the young rôles, and understudy practically everything else, and be ready for rehearsals in October. That's all that was told me that morning. So I staggered home on a bus, in a daze, excited and scared, a wage-earner, feeling immensely unready, the familiar out-lines of the future suddenly blurred by an unexpected present. I felt it was all too soon, the student days of non-responsibility and planning, suddenly foreshortened into a kind of small hell. My self-confidence collapsed.

2

Act One

The war was still on. I had met a young ace-observer from the air-force sent home from France with medals and a nervous breakdown. He seemed lost and ill and haunted our house on Long Island where we were spending the summer. My mother was going through what in those days was called discreetly her 'difficult time of life'. It seemed more difficult for everyone else than for her. My father was hard at work and I promised him to be with her as much as possible. That meant I caught an eight o'clock commuters' train to New York for my lessons every morning and was at Tanara's studio at nine, worked till twelve and managed to get home by lunch-time. This all through the summer, mostly at over ninety degrees in the shade.

It meant that Louis' weekend visits were welcome and soon my parents took him for granted. I wanted no more than walks by the sea and long talks in the evening. He had gone to Yale University before joining the air-force and was full of the new poets. One day he read to me from *Prufrock* by T.S. Eliot. Terribly avant-garde then. I was duly impressed. We listened to scratchy records that he had brought from France. But I felt there was always something hidden, some un-balance. 'The war' my parents said.

The months were rushing towards the time when re-hearsals at the Opera House would start, and I lived for that, and the kind of freedom I imagined I would find. Mother

11 As Giannetta in *L'Elisir d'Amore* at the Metropolitan Opera, 1918–19

The Metropolitan Opera
production of *Louise*

12 As the Street Gamin

13 As the Errand-girl

JEANNE GORDON
· THE FAIRY ·

MARY MELLISH
· HAPPINESS ·

FLORENCE EASTON
· THE MOTHER ·

MARY ELLIS
· MYLTYL ·

LEON ROTHIER
· THE GRANDFATHER ·

LOUISE BERAT
· THE GRANDMOTHER ·

MARGARET ROMAINE
· THE CAT ·

ROBERT COUZINOU
· THE DOG ·

RAYMONDE DELAUNOIS
· TYTYL ·

RICHARD ORDYNSKI
· STAGE DIRECTOR ·

14 From the world première programme of Albert Wolff's opera *The Blue Bird*
performed in Maeterlinck's presence at the Metropolitan Opera House,
27 December 1919

"Leah"
The Dybbuk –
New York 1925–26.

15 As Rose-Marie
in the Broadway
première of Friml's
musical play, 1924

16 As Leah in the
Neighborhood
Playhouse
production of *The
Dybbuk*, 1925

had grown consistently more hurt and depressed. I had not wanted her to practise with me because I felt, wisely, that if she accompanied me while I studied it would be at variance with what Tanara was teaching me. 'If I can't help you with my playing, I shall not play the piano at all, ever again.' And she never did. I felt guilty, of course. This all sounds as though life was on a down-beat, but it wasn't; and getting ready for that extraordinary year ahead was exciting.

October meant rehearsing almost every day at the Opera House. It was run very methodically; every available rehearsal room or space, foyers, the bars, even the roof, were used for the different casts – since eight operatic performances were given every week, seldom repeating. And at least two new operas were always in rehearsal. I was given a great deal to understudy. Assistant conductors Bamboshek and Pelletier worked at the scores, assistant stage directors mapped out the *mise-en-scène*, until everyone was ready for the full rehearsals.

On November 11th the Armistice was declared and a surge of relief and optimism swept over the country. The bells clanged, the whistles blew, parades of returning soldiers filled Fifth Avenue and crowds held up the traffic. The American people knew they had played a very important part in bringing the war to an end – but then, as in the Second World War, it was always a long-distance experience, no bombs and blitzes except for the men who had gone overseas.

On December 14th 1918 I made my début in the World Première of Puccini's triptych of operas, *Il Tabarro*, *Suor Angelica*, and *Gianni Schicchi*. The prima-donnas were Muzio, Farrar and Easton. My part was that of the young nun in *Suor Angelica*, and also to understudy Easton in *Gianni Schicchi*. The first rehearsals had been torture. But the first night made up for everything; that dead silence, after the tuning up of the orchestra, the heavy folding back of the golden damask curtain, the liveried footmen attendants who bore flowers or notes or messages from the front of house, the tier upon tier of boxes and galleries, the gleam of jewels and white shirt-fronts, the gold, the plush, the very smell of the Metropolitan, are unforgettable. Somehow the atmosphere of the splendid new opera house in the Lincoln Centre doesn't compare with that old dirty brick building, which enclosed the crimson beating heart of decades of sight and sound that spelled such enchantment.

Most of my nervousness had been during rehearsals, so I was able to be conscious, at least, at the first performances. The whole experience was so much more terrific than my own part in it that I almost enjoyed it. Not until the second season, when I was made responsible for leading parts, did my performance nerves start.

But that first year, Easton fell ill and I had to sing the leading rôle in *Schicchi* one afternoon. I fairly ate it up and the critics were very kind. Then Delaunois had a cold and I was called to sing Siebel in *Faust* at a few hours' notice. It was the weekly Tuesday night of the Opera's visit to Philadelphia – the whole company always went by train at about 3 p.m. I went over the score on the train, with conductor Monteux, got into Delaunois's tights (much *too* tight) and somehow succeeded in singing creditably without a regular rehearsal. For that effort I was presented with the rôle, and a new costume; and for three seasons I serenaded and supported fainting Marguerites with Mephistophelian troubles. One of them, fat Frances Alda, flattened me as she drooped into my arms so that Valentine picked me up, brushed me down and stood me properly in front of the soldiers' chorus, cross-sword raised to exorcise the devil and heavy prima donnas.

My friendship continued with Geraldine Farrar – I sang in Leroux's *Reine Fiammette* and Charpentier's *Louise* with her, both conducted by Monteux, and enjoyed her newly bestowed graciousness. I was scheduled to sing the Tsarevitch in *Boris* – and had gorgeous rehearsals – watching the magnificence, the absolutely colossal thrill of Chaliapin's performance. When he 'died' in my arms, his voice vibrated through my whole body, like a huge bell. He was so much larger than life, roaring and all-enveloping. I remember one evening when I was singing in Korngold's *Die tote Stadt* – Mme Jeritza, to whom he was much attached, had the dressing-room next to Delaunois's and mine. We heard him coming along the passage, so Delaunois hid in the cupboard and I behind a large armchair, while he put his head around the door and bellowed at us in Russian; there were times, just before a performance, when his golden immensity was too much, especially when tinged with vodka. I thought of those two, oversize and tawny, as two lions making love in a cage.

But to stand in the wings during *L'Elisir d'Amore* and hear Caruso sing 'Una Furtiva Lagrima' was an experience that put a seal on one's hearing. His voice was of such a tangible beauty that one could lock it up within oneself. I think being privileged to sing Gianetta in that opera, as one of 'the Four' – Barrientos and Scotti the other two – was the pinnacle for me. It wasn't a big part, but it shared the story and the glory and had a short scene in the last act with Caruso. Caruso, laughing – saying 'Mi-mi-mi' through his nose as he sucked a lozenge before he went on – Caruso, gracious, infantile – smelling of expensive eau-de-cologne – shining with kindness, and pouring out notes on an effortless breath; Caruso, never allowing one to feel small or neglected, fooling around with laughter, or insisting on another curtain-call for you, or drawing a quick caricature of somebody's face . . . Caruso, being always Caruso, whether he was Tonio, Rhadames or Pinkerton . . . somehow making you believe in the story.

Later he became very ill – he was not supposed to sing – but he did. It was *L'Elisir d'Amore* that was his last performance at the Met. in New York. Just before he went on for the final scene he handed me his handkerchief and asked me to wipe the sweat from his face; and during our duet I noticed a trickle of blood on the corner of his mouth.

METROPOLITAN OPERA HOUSE

GRAND OPERA SEASON 1918~1919
GIULIO GATTI-CASAZZA, General Manager

FRIDAY EVENING, APRIL 11TH, AT 8.15 O'CLOCK

L'ELISIR D'AMORE
(THE ELIXIR OF LOVE)

OPERA IN THREE ACTS AND FOUR SCENES

BOOK BY FELICE ROMANI

(IN ITALIAN)

MUSIC BY GAETANO DONIZETTI

ADINA	MARIA BARRIENTOS
GIANNETTA	MARY ELLIS
NEMORINO	ENRICO CARUSO
BELCORE	GIUSEPPE DE LUCA
DULCAMARA	ADAMO DIDUR
CONDUCTOR	GENNARO PAPI

STAGE DIRECTOR	RICHARD ORDYNSKI
CHORUS MASTER	GIULIO SETTI
TECHNICAL DIRECTOR	EDWARD SIEDLE
STAGE MANAGER	ARMANDO AGNINI

PROGRAMME CONTINUED ON NEXT PAGE

CORRECT LIBRETTOS FOR SALE IN THE LOBBY

HARDMAN PIANOS USED EXCLUSIVELY

He sang one more performance – I think *La Juive* in Brooklyn. And that was the end. He would not take care of himself and rest. The day after he died, rehearsals were called for his replacements. I saw the manager, Gatti-Casazza, huddled in the stalls and went up to him and said how sorry I was. He looked at me with steely eyes and said in his gutteral Italian, 'Persona è indispensabile'. It shocked me more than anything I had ever heard, and made me know how little anyone ever matters, and how every moment of living, in an instant, becomes the past.

It was getting more apparent to me that just to sing in opera, unless one had the occasional very special voice, was inadequate fulfilment. Also I saw, as I watched, that apart from Chaliapin and Scotti those who sang very well usually could not act – and those who acted well were not such fine singers. I knew that my voice would not be fully developed for another ten years or so and I was cursed with impatience – and wondered if I could work and wait that long.

My memory at this point becomes so overstacked that I endure a kind of retrospective indigestion; every phase of my life seemed to lure me into a world of different people, different behaviour, demons and angels. I was perpetually trying to adjust, to act as though all was as it should be, when I was really bewildered. I laughed easily, and this was often mistaken for acceptance, but I didn't think having my bottom pinched by elderly Latin baritones was at all funny – nor the lecherous looks from assistant German conductors who winked at each other as they discussed my springing bosom to be 'gerade eine Handvoll'. My general lack of response to these harmless back-stage vulgarities got me the nick-name of 'Vierge Marie'. Anyway, I never had any of those legendary struggles or propositionings I had been warned to expect. The approaches were always what I thought to be romantic, sometimes mutual, and alas, unfulfilled. Only once did the stage director invite me to dinner and it turned out to be an

METROPOLITAN OPERA COMPANY
METROPOLITAN OPERA HOUSE
NEW YORK

Mrs M. Ellis

You are hereby notified that the following
Rehearsal of

oris

has been scheduled for you:

Date *Monday Nov. 4*

Hour *10 30 a.m.*

Place *Stage*

With { ~~Piano~~
       Orchestra

By Order of the Management

M. Papi

REMARKS: *Chaliapin!*

invitation to his bachelor flat, candles on the table and a huge bottle of Guerlain perfume beside my plate – the evening ended with my throwing the expensive bottle at him and rushing for a taxi. I was thoroughly scared of life.

After the first season at the Opera, Louis persuaded me to marry him. So one morning Father and Mother escorted us to the City Hall in Lower Manhattan where we were married.

We went to Paris; there followed the most traumatic events ever to beset a bride, I am sure. Louis told me he longed to see his mistress of the war days. I remember her name, Marie Delorme, and even her address on the Rue Moscou. He had a photograph of her and I tried my best to look like her. I changed my hair-do and bought a hat like the one in the photograph. I would always know when he saw someone on the street, or in a café, who resembled her and finally I had the sense to tell him to go and visit her. He said that if he did not come back to the hotel by six that evening, he would be staying with her, and that we would take it from there. So I waited on a bench on the Champs Elysées that afternoon till it was time to go back to the hotel. The cars whizzed by, it was dusk and all the lights suddenly went on. The streets were filled with people, jostling, hurrying to the Metro or a bus to take them home – lovers met to sit at cafés; noise, traffic, taxi-horns, strains of distant jazz, police whistles, every sound that was Paris at the end of the day. The walk to the modest Hotel Byron was only a few yards, but it seemed to take me an hour – that bench I had been sitting on was my last certain haven.

Louis was there, in the hotel room – my joy lasted for only a second because he was in great distress, having found out that Mlle Delorme had died some months before. He was past comforting and all I could do was to be silent and let him rave and weep. Added to this he was suffering unromantically from piles, to which I had to apply some healing ointment every few hours. The Paris honeymoon was over.

As I write this I find it funny and ridiculously melo-dramatic, but to the girl I was then, it seemed like the end of the world. Louis never recovered from this, nor did I; and after watching my misery for nearly a year my father insisted that I should get a divorce and helped me over some unhappy months. Louis then married again, this time an actress of the famous Kemble-Cooper clan, who telephoned me one day to inform me that he did nothing but talk about me. Four years later I heard that he was mixed up in some scandal in Cali-fornia and had killed himself.

I was glad to have to work very hard for the second Metro-politan season. Maurice Maeterlinck had allowed his *Blue-Bird* to be made into an opera by Albert Wolff, who was also going to conduct it. Raymonde Delaunois was to sing Tyltyl, and I, Mytyl. It was a modern, difficult score. Maeterlinck himself came over from Belgium to supervise the production (he drove Ordynski, the Stage Director, half crazy and there were many Polish-Belgian fights). Maeterlinck was a big, pale man, very mischievous and vulgar despite his pompous dignity.

The first night was terrific – the boxes were full of French and Belgian Embassy officials, there were specially printed gala programmes, curtain calls, laurel wreaths, flowers, speeches, and pages and pages in the press the next day.

One day during those rehearsals, I came home to my flat and found every treasure I had collected up till then stolen. Later that year, the house next door was burned down, while I was ill and bedridden, and could not move, so that I had to listen to the screams of helpless people caught in the blaze. Still later, a famous actress, who lived in the flat above, started throwing statuary out of the window at four o'clock one morning after a wild party and was finally taken away . . . It wasn't a lucky place, to say the least.

The next new opera was Charpentier's *Louise*. Farrar sang it, and I had two comedy roles – the street urchin and the dressmaker's apprentice. During those months I had a

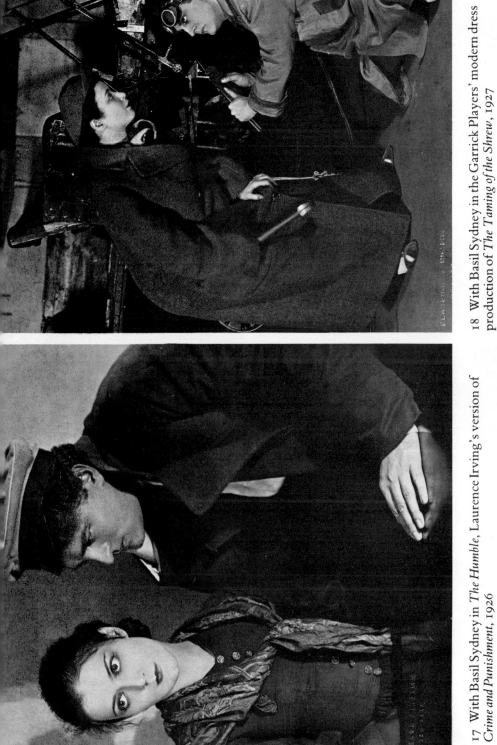

18 With Basil Sydney in the Garrick Players' modern dress production of *The Taming of the Shrew*, 1927

17 With Basil Sydney in *The Humble*, Laurence Irving's version of *Crime and Punishment*, 1926

19 David Belasco who directed me in my first Shakespearean role in *The Merchant of Venice*, Lyceum Theatre, New York, 1923

To MARY —
To PART WITH ONE YOU LOVE
is TO DIE A LITTLE
To PART WITH AN ARTIST IS TO D
VERY MUCH — milly

20 (left) Fritz Lang; 21 (above) Lewis Milestone, 'Milly', two Hollywood directors

METROPOLITAN OPERA HOUSE

GRAND OPERA SEASON 1919~1920
GIULIO GATTI-CASAZZA, General Manager

Saturday Evening, December 27th, at 8 o'clock

SPECIAL PERFORMANCE

UNDER THE AUSPICES OF

THE INTERALLIED ART ASSOCIATION

Patrons: Their Majesties
The KING and QUEEN of BELGIUM
AND THE
PRESIDENT of the FRENCH REPUBLIC
FOR THE BENEFIT OF
The Queen of Belgium Fund, Millerand Fund for French Children
The Three Big Sisters Organizations (Catholic, Protestant, Jewish)
Milk for Children of America

WORLD PREMIERE

THE BLUE BIRD
(L'OISEAU BLEU)

Fairy Opera IN FRENCH, in Four Acts and Eight Tableaux

Book by MAURICE MAETERLINCK.   Music by ALBERT WOLFF

Tyltyl .... Raymonde Delaunois	The Joy of Seeing What Is Beautiful, Cecil Arden
Mytyl .... Mary Ellis	The Fairy .... Jeanne Gordon
Mummy Tyl .... Florence Easton	The Night .... Frances Ingram
Daddy Tyl .... Paolo Ananian	The Cat .... Margaret Romaine
Granny Tyl .... Louise Berat	The Dog .... Robert Couzinou
Gaffer Tyl .... Leon Rothier	Neighbour Berlingot ...... Jeanne Gordon
The Maternal Love ..... Florence Easton	Happiness .... Mary Mellisn
The Joy of Understanding. Gladys Axman	A Child .... Adelina Vosari
Light .... Flora Perini	Milk .... Marie Tiffany
Father Time .... Leon Rothier	Water .... Adelina Vosari
Bread .... Mario Laurenti	Sugar .... Octave Dua
The Little Girl .... Edna Kellogg	Fire .... Angelo Bada
The Little Lovers .... } Minnie Egener } Helena Marsh	Children, Misses Belleri, Borniggia, Florence,
The Joy of Being Just.. Margaret Farnam	Kennedy, Manetti, Stabe, White.

Conducted by the Composer

PROGRAMME CONTINUED ON NEXT PAGE

CORRECT LIBRETTOS FOR SALE IN THE LOBBY   HARDMAN PIANOS USED EXCLUSIVELY letter from David Belasco, the theatre producer, writer and director, asking me to go and see him. When I did, he told me that he had been watching me for two years and suggested that when I finished my opera contract I should devote myself to the straight theatre, as he thought he could make an actress out of me, making it clear that it would be a long time before I was able to do the rôles I wanted to do.

My life had been all music up till then and, although all aspects of the theatre thrilled me; I hadn't seriously thought of existence without singing. Belasco had the wiles of the devil, and I knew it, but at twenty-one one doesn't reason very soundly.

All those years of study didn't seem to matter . . . it was the *theatre* that bewitched me – the backstage workings and tension; the expectant hush; the impersonal hunger that somehow surged across the footlights from that greedy animal, the audience.

After three years at the Opera I seemed to have lost a sense of humour. Living with a voice and an ambition was rather like living with a race-horse. There could be no relaxation and, of course, perpetual practise and care and early hours. I must have been a terrible bore. I always made my mother leave me well before we reached the stage-door, so 'they' wouldn't think I was perpetually chaperoned. Even so, rumours got about; and I remember a drive in the Park with Miss Farrar, when she admonished me for something that hadn't happened and that I knew nothing about. I was more shocked that she could believe I was even interested in some dreary oily Italian baritone, than at the apparent fact that someone was making up stories about me. In fact I think I must have been a deadly prig at that time and I probably missed a lot of fun. Or did I? There were a few young women who had started the same season – but we sang in different operas, so I couldn't compare notes.

Two very amusing happenings stand out in my memory.

There was an ambitious young Italian, who finally came to sing the small part of the doctor in the last act of *Traviata*. At a matinée he was so nervous when at last his one or two phrases of singing occurred that he forgot his words and lost his voice and all he could do, to tell the waiting audience how Violetta was getting on, was to make a vague Latin gesture of doubt with his hand, before scuttling back into the wings, from where, I presume, he never emerged again. Then there was the famous matinée of an opera in English. It was all about the Crusades, and in a great scene there was a tread-mill with, seemingly, hundreds of crusaders in coats of mail, marching past. Unfortunately, one poor little man in the chorus got wedged between two great shields and unmistakeably he came marching past again, his wrinkled 'chain-mail' tights slipping lower and lower each time round – and the audience getting hysterical. The conductor finally put down his baton until the march was over.

In opera one is invited to show individuality in a part and, as long as the music remains perfectly within its frame, the more excitement and personal creativeness that is brought to a rôle, the better. Example: Jeritza, lying on the floor to sing 'Vissi d'arte' in *Tosca*. The floor had never been used before. In those days most singers did not like even to sit down to sing, much less lie down. I think it was this that made Geraldine Farrar decide to retire. I suppose many have sung better than Farrar; but it did not matter; she created the perfect illusion that it was necessary to sing at given moments, just as Callas did many years later – Mary Garden too, but I heard her only a few times. Her voice was not always pleasant, but *Le Jongleur de Notre Dame* was something never to be forgotten, even though her French was atrocious.

I went to many concerts on free evenings; and loved watching Leopold Stokowski, remembering the first time I had seen him walking down that mountain in Switzerland, his loden-cape flying, looking free and happy; but Toscanini remained for me the supreme conductor of them all. Nor has there been anyone since to match him.

Then Geraldine Farrar left the Opera House – her farewell performance was almost a riot. The 'Gerry-Flappers' behaved very much like the pop-star fans of today – screams and tears and applause. A great wave of glamour left the Opera House with her.

There was still a season before me at the Met.; the same old operas, the same parts, the same rehearsals, fears of catching cold, gossip, and singers' bitchery. I was glad when it was over.

*   *   *

Before I left the Opera I had signed with David Belasco to appear as Nerissa in *The Merchant of Venice*, which was to be a huge production for the star David Warfield. In my meetings with him I was overwhelmed by Belasco's personality, his rather adamant gentleness, and would have walked a tight-rope had he asked me to. Before I started rehearsing for him, he insisted, and indeed arranged it, that I should go for six months to a stock company in Indianapolis – a town in the middle west, which had a company the equivalent of the Liverpool and Birmingham repertory companies in England. It was directed by an extraordinary man named Stuart Walker, and I think almost every reputable player in America had at some time worked for him.

So, with great excitement one spring day, I packed a trunk, bought a large supply of make-up and sped westwards; I was to get the sum of ten dollars weekly, play a different part every week and supply my own costumes, except for the period plays. I landed at an apartment-hotel called the Spink Arms. The Murat Theatre was huge and old-fashioned. I was in a strange town without friends, without a piano, without a clue as to what was ahead of me. The Opera House, the music, the glamour, seemed a dream already. I could offer no excuse for what I was doing to myself, or to my baffled parents and friends. I was alone, a student again, getting no money to speak of. When I think of it now, I simply cannot understand what made me leave what was an assured career to start afresh; why I was willing to forget singing – how I had the courage to push aside what little I had achieved, and all the years of hard study, to find myself in mid-summer with the temperature over ninety in the shade, sitting in a cold bath half the night learning lines for next week's play. Well, that summer taught me a lot. I learned to accomplish in one reading the outline of a character, to memorise pages of script in five days and, by the time I got to the sixth week or so, my brain was a jungle – but on it went! And on went the violent heat, the changing and sewing of costumes; even the making of a cotton-wool wig, sprinkled with Christmas tinsel-powder, for *The School for Scandal*! And on went the work, nourished by a daily telegram from Mr Belasco. I am sure he did this to all his young artists but every morning before I went to rehearsal, there was a message under my door urging me to work well and counting the days until my return and the rehearsals with him for *The Merchant of Venice*. At that time he also sent me a script – his own translation of a Guitry play, *La Petite Main qui se Place* which he said I was to do after playing Nerissa. I realise now it was a wily bait to keep me alert and alive, but, then, it beckoned me on, no matter how discouraged and tired I was.

I can hardly remember Indianapolis – only the street from the Spink Arms to the theatre and one private house of a charming lady who befriended me; I think her name was Rosa and she watched my progress and was kind. Of course I met, but hardly knew, the players there. We were all so beset with work. The girls were left to themselves – we walked home every night while all the 'boys', with Mr Walker, passed us in a great open car. No comment.

Some of the plays were very well done; others I was frankly ashamed to be in, but every production had quality of a sort and I didn't miss the opera at all. I felt a sort of justification – I had fallen into the opera so easily, so unexpectedly; but this was hard and unrewarding – a kind of penance. Then, I didn't realise that talent always carried its labour with ease, and I need not have had a conscience about the seasons at the opera seeming too happy. Later on, in certain plays that were right, and that I played well, I felt the same happiness. Perhaps it was a certain rigorous upbringing that made me feel guilty when I enjoyed work too much. Anyway that summer was a wholesome dose of painful, and I think now, rather futile labour.

All the magic came back a hundred-fold when rehearsals for *The Merchant of Venice* started in New York. No-one in the theatre today can imagine what Mr Belasco demanded. He was an extraordinary man, always dressed in black, with a clerical collar, white hair above an almost feminine face – black eyes with an arrow of light in them. He had an amazing history in the theatre – he made many American stars. He was responsible for many plays, the writing and the adaptation of them, and the librettos of operas – Puccini's *Madame Butterfly* and *Girl of the Golden West* were his. His eccentricities were not affectation – they were all an absolute expression of himself. His flat, on top of the Belasco Theatre, was a museum of collectors' pieces, chiefly of the Napoleonic era. A religious aura hung over everything, too; crosses, stained glass, rosaries, candles, vestments – all of this lit by hidden spotlights.

Supper with him was more theatrical than any of his productions; there would always be gifts, and surprises. He was a superb showman and an indefatigable worker. Always planning a production, or writing – sometimes passing the whole day in pyjamas and dressing-gown – with a drive in the park at night, and champagne to stimulate him. His theatre was a sanctum – back-stage there was an unbreakable rule of silence; stage hands had to wear plimsolls and white cotton gloves when handling delicate scenery, while rolls of thick carpet were put down behind the sets to muffle all footsteps.

Not only were the rules strict, but he instilled into everyone a complete respect for the job. We lunched, and often supped in the theatre, in a great rehearsal green-room under the stage. He sat at the head of the long table, talking about the theatre, the production, never letting us have contact with the outer world. Sending the cast home in cars – showing every possible consideration, making life easy, artistically and financially, in return for undivided loyalty and attention to him and the work in hand. Telling gorgeous stories of the theatre in America from its pioneer days – his black eyes sparkling whenever he mentioned some enchantress that he had known.

Mary Servoss was playing Portia, a young actress who had never had much of a chance. Lovely she was, with beautiful red-gold hair. David Warfield was an over-sympathy-squeezing Shylock, Philip Merrivale a beautiful Basanio. The costumes were made in Paris, each weighing a ton and to do quick-change, between the scenes while one counted up to seventy, was agony. We all lived in a perpetual state of excitement, so that I cannot remember my family or friends, or anything during those months. Of course my mother and father were all against my leaving the Opera. I suppose they felt it was more respectable and serious than the theatre, plus the fact that they had helped me for years to accomplish that first goal. My behaviour must have been inexplicable to them, then. It's too late, now, to say that I am sorry.

We went on a tour prior to opening in New York. To travel with a Belasco production of that size meant three special coaches on the train, our rooms and meals all ordered for us: supper with him every night, usually cold ham, salad, and a baked apple. Nothing to drink except, for special occasions, champagne. Belasco always said: 'If a woman never drinks or smokes, she will remain young and beautiful till she is ninety.' Well – I feel exceedingly young. When we came back from tour, it was like being torn away from a family – I walked into

Lyceum Theatre

West 45th Street, Near Broadway.
NEW LYCEUM THEATRE COMPANY, - OWNERS
DANIEL FROHMAN, - - - - PRESIDENT
CHARLES FROHMAN, INC. and DAVID BELASCO,
Lessees and Managers.

NOTICE: This Theatre, with every seat occupied, can be emptied in less than three minutes. Choose NOW the Exit nearest to your seat, and in case of fire walk (do not run) to that Exit.

THOMAS J. DRENNAN, Fire Commissioner.

WEEK BEGINNING MONDAY EVENING, FEBRUARY 26, 1923

Matinees Thursday and Saturday

DAVID BELASCO

Presents

MR. WARFIELD

As SHYLOCK

—in—

WM. SHAKESPEARE'S

The Merchant of Venice

The Characters as Cast

DUKE OF VENICE...............................A. E. Anson
PRINCE OF MOROCCO......................Reginald Goode
ANTONIO, the Merchant.......................Ian MacLaren
BASSANIO, his kinsmn and friend...............Philip Merivale
GRATIANO ....) .....W. I. Percival
LORENZO .... | Friends to } ....Horace Braham
SALARINO .... } Antonio and Bassanio } ....Herbert Ranson
SOLANIO ....) ..Edward Crandall
SHYLOCK, the Jew.......................DAVID WARFIELD
TUBAL ....) Countrymen and } ....Albert Bruning
CHUS .... { Friends to Shylock } ..Morris Strassberg
LAUNCELOT GOBBO, Servant to Shylock........Percival Vivian
OLD GOBBO, father to Launcelot...............Fuller Mellish
BALTHAZAR, Steward to Portia...............Charles Harbury
STEPHANO, a servant to Portia............... Philip Bender
LEONARDO, a servant to Bassanio.........St. Julian Fowlkes
A JESTER, at Belmont.......................Warde de Wolfe
CLERK OF THE COURT.........................Nick Long
A DUCAL MESSENGER......................Michael Welansky
PORTIA, a rich heiress.......................Mary Servoss
NERISSA, her waiting gentlewoman.................Mary Ellis
JESSICA, daughter to Shylock.....................Julia Adler

Magnificoes of Venice; Officers of the Court of Justice; Gentlemen and Gentlewomen; Citizens of Venice; Jews; Servants and others.

PERIOD—About the First Quarter of the Sixteenth Century.

PLACE—In Italy: Partly in Venice, and partly at Belmont—the country seat of Portia, upon the neighboring mainland.

my little flat, and found that Belasco had ordered it to be re-decorated while I was away. What could one say about such generosity? He was the same with everyone; if one worked well and he liked one – and I cannot remember anyone he didn't like – nothing was too much for him to do.

He usually knew unerringly what the public wanted – but in *The Merchant of Venice* his judgement failed him. He attacked the play unclassically. New York had been used to its Shakespeare elocuted by Sothern and Marlowe, and decorated as they had always seen it. Here were actors who were not Shakespearean, young women, beautiful in Venetian dresses designed by a master-Frenchman – a carnival spirit of comedy – except for the over-pathetic Shylock; it was too much to expect the public and critics to swallow. It ran for several months and gave me an experience the like of which I have never had again. But its failure broke Belasco's heart – or at least chipped it.

During that winter, I received two memorable visits. The first was one afternoon – or evening, I'm not sure which – when a young man, slender and shy, came to see me. I cannot remember why he came, or who sent him. But he played the piano – and sang – and I gave him a sandwich; and I remember a vague sadness when he left. I did not see him again for many years, and when I did he was still young, attractive and clever, but Noel Coward was no longer shy. The second was one evening, very late, when Geraldine Farrar came to see me. She had heard I was to marry again and came to beg me not to do so and to consider the step very seriously. I wish I had listened to her. It turned out a disastrous thing for me to have done. But a Byronic young man Edwin Knopf, an actor, had come into my life. I was very fond of him, but refused to marry him and he went abroad, to Germany. While there he had a dreadful accident; some kind of 'snow-bomb' exploded and he lost his hand and part of his arm. I felt responsible somehow and when he returned I married him, and I hope helped in readjusting his life and making him overcome any disability. But that wasn't enough and it didn't work out. I behaved very badly and I have always been sorry and ashamed. The only good thing that came of it was his subsequent marriage to a lovely young woman who had been my friend. So it ended happily for him, anyway.

After the Belasco-Shakespeare experience, Gilbert Miller engaged me for a part in a bad play called *Casanova* (aren't all plays about him impossible?) This one at least had Katharine Cornell in her first leading part, but nothing could help Lowell Sherman find his way into the eighteenth century.

While it was on, Henry Miller, Gilbert's father, and one of the grand old gentlemen of the theatre, asked me to play in *The Merry Wives of Gotham* – also a costume play, chiefly concerned with the Irish squatters in the nineties 'in New York. Victor Herbert wrote his last song 'Singing in the Rain' for it, which I sang; I'm afraid my brogue was awful, but I did what I could.

One evening during this play Arthur Hammerstein sat in the second row of the stalls. It meant nothing to me to hear of it that evening – but I soon received a call to go and see him. At his office I met Rudolf Friml, the composer, and Oscar Hammerstein II, then a big, gentle, very young man. At that meeting *Rose Marie* was born. They all persuaded me that I must sing again and told me that what they had in mind was a new kind of play with a really dramatic story and fine music which would demand real singing – more like an Offenbach light opera. It was to be the first of Oscar's long list of timeless musical plays. It was about a French Canadian girl and her love for Jim, a fur trapper, wrongly accused of murder. Hammerstein got Dennis King to play him. Dennis had been having a Shakespearean season in New York and no-one then knew he had a splendid baritone voice. After *Rose Marie* he swashbuckled and sang in Friml's two later musicals *The Three Musketeers* and *The Vagabond King*.

Friml was tireless and composed song after song as Oscar's lyrics took shape, with Harbach helping, and scenes were written. *Rose Marie* is now famous but how can anyone who was not closely involved then appreciate what work and love and excitement went into it? It is hard for me to realise now that it was for me and I am still very proud that it was. I was not conscious then of my great good fortune – perhaps we never are at the time.

Day by day the production grew and, before I knew what was happening, rehearsals were in full swing. I felt dim and awful because I knew none of the ways and means of operetta. I bought French-Canadian books of poetry and learned the Canuck accent, and plunged into the playing with all the zeal of attacking Sardou and Puccini rolled into one! Perhaps that ultimately came over and accounted partly for its extravagant and phenomenal success. It is still something I cannot understand because, in the pre-New York tour that summer, we felt too terrible for words and managed to see only the long grim faces of the management in that try-out.

We were in Long Branch – a famous sea-side try-out place. The only hotel Dennis and I could get into was a kosher Jewish one, where we were fed on cucumbers and sour cream, among other things, which almost killed me with violent indigestion and added to a depression that seemed ominous. The ocean looked inviting enough to walk into and so avoid the terror of the New York opening.

On September 2nd 1924 at the Imperial Theatre, *Rose Marie* and the 'Indian Love Call' became theatre history. All I remember of that first night is sitting cross-legged on the table in Act One and reaching a pianissimo high B-flat which brought the house down. After that, euphoria, bliss and the final curtain fulfilling everyone's expectations. During the run, Sir Alfred Butt asked me to go to England to play Rose Marie at Drury Lane. But for some reason I refused and the part was played in London by Edith Day. It is strange to think

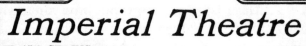

Imperial Theatre

249 W. 45th ST., INC.. OWNERS
LEE and J. J. SHUBERT
S. H. STONE ....
A. H. PINCUS .... } .... DIRECTORS
M. L. GOLDSTONE .....

NOTICE: This Theatre, with every seat occupied, can be emptied in less than three minutes. Choose NOW the Exit nearest to your seat, and in case of fire walk (do not run) to that Exit.
THOMAS J. DRENNAN, Fire Commissioner.

WEEK BEGINNING MONDAY EVENING, DECEMBER 22, 1924
Matinees Wednesday, Thursday, Friday and Saturday

ARTHUR HAMMERSTEIN
Presents

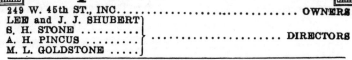

"ROSE-MARIE"

A Musical Play With

MARY ELLIS

And a Broadway Cast Including

WILLIAM KENT   DENNIS KING

Book and Lyrics by Otto Harbach   Music by Rudolf Friml and
and Oscar Hammerstein 2nd   Herbert Stothart
Dances Arranged by David Bennett   Book Staged by Paul Dickey
Gowns and Costumes Designed by Charles Le Maire
Settings by Gates and Morange
Production Under Personal Supervision of Arthur Hammerstein
Orchestra Under Direction of Rupert Graves
The Cast
(Characters as they appear)
SERGEANT MALONE.......................ARTHUR DEAGON
LADY JANE.............................DOROTHY MACKAYE

PROGRAM CONTINUED ON SECOND PAGE FOLLOWING

that I might have been in Drury Lane in 1925, instead of ten years later when I was destined to perform there!

All sorts of good things happened during that run of *Rose Marie*. I re-met one of my life-long friends, Romney Brent. I had first met him when he was with the Theatre Guild Company. Born in Mexico with the lilting name of Romulo Laralde, he became best known in comedy and was the original singer of Noel Coward's 'Mad Dogs and English-men'. He often told me later that he remembered coming back to my dressing room after the first night of *Rose Marie* and that I had on an unglamorous pink and white striped bath-robe and seemed in a daze. I met Basil Sydney with him later. Basil, whose tremendous theatre knowledge helped to make me realise how ultimately tiring plays with music are – and how much better a good straight play, which can be *re-created* at every performance . . . according to the audience and the actor's intelligence.

After the theatre there were supper parties. There was a small group of us: George Gershwin, Romney, Fred and Adele Astaire, Margarita D'Alvarez – rather like a Velasquez duenna to us all – Heifetz and his beautiful sister Pauline and Harpo Marx. George Gershwin was already very successful – the Astaires were appearing in his *Lady Be Good* on Broadway. George never changed – he was completely music-geared and a warm reticent being. Harpo was solid and intelligent and it was difficult to imagine that sober young man as the zany harpist. Heifetz seemed in another world – on a higher ledge of professionalism – but we were all mad and in love with life and work, and each other.

I had a bad throat for several days and George came and played all the new bits of *Rhapsody in Blue* which he was composing. I shall never forget sitting in bed, with the door open through to the living-room, where he at the piano was trying over that haunting melody of the second part of the Rhapsody. That year he gave me a copy of the first edition for

Christmas, bound in purple suede, with 'To Mary' stamped in
gold on the cover. Pauline got one too! On New Year's Day,
after an all-night party, we all listened to Heifetz playing Bach
as I have never heard it played since. At five in the morning I
went to bed for a few hours, then got up to sing a matinée and
evening performance. I adored Gershwin, but George was in
love with Pauline Heifetz. And so that hectic, working winter
of 1924 went by; it is difficult to recapture, even in thought,
the energy, the spirit of that group of young people . . . all of
us striving in our own way, plunging towards the future – but
then the present was enough, and friendship and hard work
and music – all kinds of music – from Heifetz's Bach, and
Harpo's harp, to Astaire's tapping feet.

Carl Van Vechten and his wife had a flat below me. They
were gatherers of 'artists' and both interesting individuals. He
was a writer, a cat-lover, a Harlem enthusiast. She, the
Russian actress Fania Marinoff. One evening they had a
small party; Gershwin, Paul Robeson, Margarita D'Alvarez
and me. George said: 'Here's a new song', and the three of us
sang 'Someday he'll come along, the man I love'. I defy any
composer to get a better first hearing than that. It was fun.

There are times in everyone's life when the unpredictable in
one's own behaviour seems to take over. Such a period came
after *Rose Marie* had been running for more than a year.
Thinking of it now, I cannot understand the courage that
prompted me to say I'd had enough, and to leave the bright
lights and all they meant to join an Art Theatre in an out of the
way down-town district, the Jewish ghetto in fact. At first I
claimed tiredness – this may have been true enough – but I
cannot imagine anything but a psychological reason for such
intense weariness. A throat specialist agreed that my voice
was tired, so I persuaded Arthur Hammerstein to let me leave
Rose Marie. He did so, but made me sign an injunction which
prevented me from singing for any management but his. That
meant that I never sang in the United States again.

*   *   *

So in 1925 I played Leah in the Neighbourhood Playhouse's wonderful production of *The Dybbuk*. This was a professional theatre centre, run by the dedicated Lewisohn Sisters. They invited the director of the 'Habima' Theatre over to direct the play. It was a strange, romantic story of Jewish folk-lore. It tells how a girl's lover dies and his spirit enters her body so that she speaks in his voice. The religious trial scene, the exorcism and then her death, were of a challenging beauty. It ran for months – and I don't think I've ever been prouder of doing a play. After the understandable acidity in the press about my leaving *Rose Marie*, it was doubly exciting to feel justified and to have their unstinted blessing. Everything fell into place. I was absolutely happy.

My salary amounted to very little, but the theatre was packed for every performance. So the management then put on Martinez Sierras' *The Romantic Young Lady* to alternate with it, and the Spanish comedy was a healthy contrast.

While *The Dybbuk* was on, the famous Moscow Arts Theatre, and the Moscow Musical Art Theatre headed by Stanislavsky and Nemerovitch Dantchenko were taking New York by storm. Their productions were magical. Both companies came to a special performance at the Playhouse and gave us a party afterwards. At that party for *The Dybbuk* Dantchenko said that if I learned Russian (I have been trying to ever since, on and off!) I could come and stay and play with them for a season. Whether he meant it or not doesn't matter; at that moment it was like giving me a pair of wings.

The particular magic of Chekhov was captured years later by the St Denis' production in London of *Three Sisters*, but it always seems to me that productions of Russian plays in English are loaded down – just as French comedies are made too trivial, too farcical – a strange imbalance, perhaps because of the translation.

In the Moscow Theatre Company was Maria Ouspenskaya, who later went to Hollywood and played many character parts with great fervour. Before she went westward, she taught for several years in New York, and many of us took lessons from her. She was a magnificent teacher, if you could take it, full of a sarcasm and biting criticism. I remember vividly every lesson with her and still benefit from them. For instance, before I was permitted to learn a line of Nina in Chekhov's *The Seagull*, she made me write a copy-book full of Nina's life from her infancy up to the time the play opened – this was called 'long distance mood' . . . It may sound strange and affected, but it was not and her attack on a part was as sound and sure as a perfect note of music.

Ouspenskaya told us how the Moscow Art Theatre Company lived together and studied their plays for years, in summer at a big Dacha in the country, living like one family, growing to know every idiosyncracy of their actor-egos. She had escaped from the Revolution. She was still a fairly young woman, but her physical ordeal had left her grey-haired and sans teeth, and yet sparkling with energy and able to translate to all of us, who were lucky enough to know her, a courage and an excitement that were contagious.

The part that I played much later in Terence Rattigan's one hour play, *The Browning Version*, benefited most from her teaching because I had to create a background and a character in such a very short playing time.

All sorts of things happened that year. Basil Sydney was playing the modern dress *Hamlet* at the Booth Theatre; and I think his was the most intelligent *Hamlet* I've ever listened to. I have been moved more emotionally – by Moissi and Gielgud – but never was the *meaning* of Shakespeare's words made so clear as when spoken by Basil. I worked away endlessly that season to know more and more about every facet of the theatre; production for me was as exciting as performance. That has remained with me, often to my chagrin, because it can be, and has been, misunderstood and my general enthusiasm in the theatre has been taken to be 'not minding my own business' which was supposed to be acting and nothing else.

22 & 23 My first appearance on the London stage at the Ambassadors Theatre in *Knave and Quean* with Robert Donat, 1930

25 With, left to right, Basil Sydney, Ralph Morgan and D. MacDonald in Eugene O'Neill's *Strange Interlude*, Lyric Theatre, London, 1931

24 Crossing the Atlantic on the *Bremen* with Basil Sydney, 1930

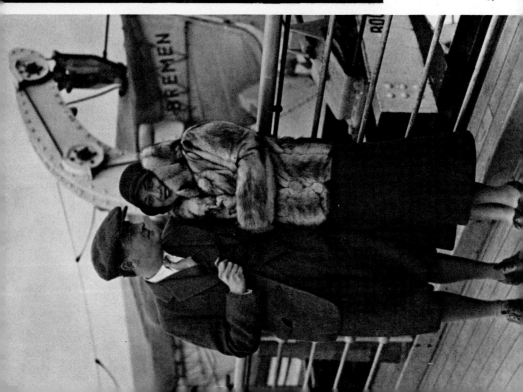

I've always believed that the more one knows about everything, the better. Not only the related arts, but a general
knowledge . . . It sounds pompous and intolerant perhaps,
but I cannot imagine anyone being an artist in one way and not
having some discrimination about everything. It is different
with the purely native talents. An instinctive acting talent can
be inherent in a completely insensitive human being – or a
purely egocentric one. But all knowledge is surely related to
what one is doing: though there will never be enough time to
read everything, see everything, hear everything.

While I was at the Playhouse I had more time, because work
was so definitely set for months. I translated several plays that
year – two Italian ones, *Death Takes a Holiday*, and one by Sam
Benelli and some German ones including, *Duell am Lido*
which had exactly the same theme as Noel Coward's *Design
for Living*, years later.

As *The Dybbuk* was drawing to an end, Basil Sydney and I
decided to begin acting together and the autumn of 1926 saw
our first partnership in Laurence Irving's version of Dostoi-
evsky's *Crime and Punishment*. That was the start of six
wonderful years of work, plays, production, and all the
worries of really learning the job of the theatre. Basil was a
perfectionist and was often found difficult for that reason; but
I respected and trusted him completely and so those years
were the most beneficial in my career. We had wonderful
friends: authors, artists, producers. We lived in half-a-house
with a garden, far over on the East Side on Sixty-Second
Street, and I think Basil was prouder then of growing a
Talisman rose in a New York back-yard than of our having
had the Success of the Season, 1927, in his production of *The
Taming of the Shrew*. It was the longest consecutive run of a
Shakespeare play ever – thirty-two weeks. They called us The
Garrick Players, because by then we had taken over the old
Garrick Theatre when the Theatre Guild moved to its new
home on Fifty-Second Street.

That summer we were invited to do the first season at the
Newport Casino. It was the beginning of the now-famous
'Summer Circuit'. Newport, Rhode Island was the play-
ground of millionaires and of so-called 'High Society', the
whole business a hundred times more class-conscious than
any caricature of the English social system. With some it was
'old' families (they couldn't be older than their arrival with the
Pilgrim Fathers anyway) but mostly it was money that was
the yard-stick. The actors were allowed to go through the
Casino grounds to the theatre, but *not* allowed to use their
bathing beach! We were fêted at dinners and parties, but
hardly acknowledged in casual meetings. There was not much
chance for casual meeting anyway, or sea and sunbathing.

Basil and I lived at a small hotel. Roses grew in profusion in
hedges on the sea-cliff walk. I never knew before that salty air
made roses more fragrant. We made many friends, but I felt
weirdly out of key – rather like a paid court-jester.

The rehearsals and performances kept us busy, though we
tried to do mainly plays we knew – from Shakespeare and
Shaw to French farce. But one glorious Sunday we were the
guests at the Moses Taylors' in their beautiful house. The
early lunch was served from gold-plated dishes – I shall never
forget the incongruity of sausages and pancakes offered in this
way. And afterwards we went to the stables to see some
magnificent Arabian horses.

This day, and many other fantastic ones, punctuated that
strange summer. I remember a huge evening party given by
Mrs Brokaw (later famous as Clare Booth Luce), very beautiful and blonde. Looking at it from here and now, it seems like
a Hollywood extravanganza, totally unreal, and unnecessary.

The Garrick Players were a gratifying success. How much
money we made or lost I shall never know – I was only
interested in the working end of things – but critics and public
supported us nobly. *The Taming of the Shrew* had been jointly
produced by H.K. Ayliff and Basil, and it caused a sensation. It

was in modern dress, with not a line changed or omitted, and even the Christopher Sly sequences kept in. Old Sly and his young friend sat in the centre of the first row at every performance – shocking whatever old ladies happened to find themselves next to him at the matinées. The critics were for the most part ecstatic, and it had a very long run.

I was in such a state of nerves that the day after the opening I was convinced we had a failure and it took me a week to realise that it was a tremendous hit, although something of a shock to Shakespeare-ites. Maria Ouspenskaya was playing Curtis (it is usually played by an old man) and Petruchio's 'Come on, in God's name' was said as he cranked an old Ford on the road homewards. Nothing one writes or remembers can possibly describe the gaiety, the freshness and edge of that production. We put on, to alternate with it, Bruno Frank's play *Twelve Thousand* and did it in perfect eighteenth-century manner – as if to challenge the very few who found our stylised *Shrew* too much for them.

The next play we did was a translation from the Hungarian by Zoe Akins – a drama about the Mayerling story – so I read all about tragic Marie Vetsera. Basil Sydney was Rudolf; Henry Stevenson the Austrian Emperor; all ending in a nice double suicide and based on *one* of the Mayerling theories, that poor Marie was sent back to Vienna, a corpse sitting up in the corner of a closed carriage. I liked the last moment when Mr Cleugh, dressed in royal footman's uniform, carried me offstage, presumably to the waiting barouche.

I had almost been carried off completely during the run of the play. We had to drink several glasses of 'champagne' in the last scene. Of course, this is never the real thing – usually ginger ale or cold tea; in this case the props man had given us cider every night and after a few weeks I was in a state of colic – the doctor couldn't make out why – but all was discovered in time to keep me from dissolving.

About this time, the 'talkies' were attracting the theatre

stars and Basil and I were called to do a test for Fox. Albert
Parker, a right-hand man for Fox Films, arranged that we
should do a scene from *The Devil's Disciple* by Shaw and that I
should sing a song. I chose Schubert's 'Who is Sylvia?' not
realising that it was supposed to be a jinx to sing that, just as
quoting *Macbeth* is supposed to be bad luck in the theatre. It
was bad luck in a strangely negative sense. The test was
evidently good. I was offered a contract, but Basil was not, so I
did not accept. Al Parker became one of the most successful
artists' representatives in London and he never forgot what he
called my 'sacrifice'. It didn't seem so to me. All through my
life I've missed opportunities because of human relationships
and I've tried very hard never to regret anything I haven't
done, but sometimes I wonder. In this instance my whole
life-style would have changed.

There followed a bad period – a very hot summer, no work,
and very little money. We used to take the crowded, literally
stinking Long Island train in the morning to the sea, get cool,
and arrive back in a torrid New York to sizzle and worry. But
somehow, worry did not persist. Fortunately one remembers
unpleasantness as little as one remembers physical pain. When
it is over, there is no way to imagine it – only the results
remain: a fear, a defence, an inhibition.

My parents had been very unhappy about me, which didn't
help matters. In those days the idea of two young people
living together was one of the unthinkable things to happen in
a respectable family, so not a day passed when my mother
didn't weep and say 'What can I tell my friends?' So at the end
of *The Taming of the Shrew* Basil and I spent a weekend with
Ouspenskaya, up in New Milford, Connecticut, and knocked
at a minister's door, and he married us. We knew that it was an
unwise thing to have done. Basil hated the idea of what he
called a shot-gun wedding, especially when it was my mother
who was holding the gun. Then back to New York, work,
and friends, and an uneasy truce with my parents. There were

hilarious evenings to balance depressing days. I learned to cook well and our funny garden apartment was open house to our old friends, and to many new ones; one, Captain Perfyelief, painter-cum-Cossack, a white Russian who had spent months with the monks on Mount Athos painting their portraits, was a remarkable story-teller (in every sense of the word) and of terrific strength.

One evening he stood between Roland Young and Basil, took each by the hand and, with a turn of the wrist, flipped them upside down and around, as though they were pancakes. At least, that is how I remember it – but we had had Bacardi rum with our pineapple juice! He could also put a match on the edge of the table and cut it in two with a sabre, without marking the polish on the table.

Then there was the Dennis family. Beautiful Lilla had been a singer; she had four sons and a benign husband. The whole family were devoted friends and we spent many wonderful times with them. It was Lilla who came over from America just to be with me on the night *Glamorous Night* opened at Drury Lane. And all through these years I felt her friendship, even though we met very seldom. She was one of the few people who fulfilled her outer beauty with inner grace. The weekends at her house were a cosy change of tempo.

Basil and I were constantly reading new plays – Eugene O'Neill, Philip Barry, Robert Sherwood, among the many. We clung to the idea of acting together and while it lasted it was good, if limiting.

Then in February 1929 came a play of A.A. Milne's. In England it had been called *To Have The Honour*, but we called it by its original title, *To Meet The Prince*. It was very light and unimportant, but it was my first real link with the English theatre.

At about this time I met Constance Collier. I had seen her playing in *Peter Ibbetson* years before with John Barrymore. I shall never forget the first visit I paid her. She had a suite at the famous Algonquin Hotel, complete with maid-secretary Phyllis, a dog, a monkey, a refrigerator and a portable gramophone. All these things (except Phyllis who made the tea) seemed strewn about the room. I sat shyly on the end of her bed, while she rested and received me with royal condescension. I was fascinated by her wit and her voice, and her great warmth and later, when I came to work in England, she was most welcoming and kind. That New York afternoon the monkey accidentally sat on the upturned arm of the portable gramophone open on the floor; and its needle surely killed any love of music that he might have had. He jumped sky high and ran up the curtains where he sat chattering, enraged, on the pelmet, refusing to come down. Miss Collier called the porter, the bell-boys, the head-waiter, the management. In the pandemonium, I escaped.

I walked up Fifth Avenue in the winter twilight. In those days, there was nothing more exciting – the sharp air, the brightly lit windows, the skyscrapers towering and etched against a cloudless dark blue sky; Childs, a cafeteria where one could get waffles and maple syrup, baked apple and coffee after the theatre and then stroll slowly and safely home at midnight; the quiet Fifth Avenue buses gliding by, half-empty; stopping to look in Tiffany's window ablaze with jewels, at the dresses one couldn't afford displayed in Saks, Bergdorff Goodman, Tappé, and Bendel's windows; the whole of Fifty-Seventh Street full of shops and art galleries; Carnegie Hall emptying a late concert audience, most of whom went next door to the Russian Tea-Room restaurant for bortsch and blinis and caviar. A whole party of young people might dance homewards after an evening out; the girls in white fox fur capes and little sequined skull-caps; the young men uncomfortable in stiff shirt-fronts, sh-sh-ing the girls who sang snatches of jazz into the amplifying night air. And in front of the Plaza, in the moonlight, the thin sleepy horses and fat coachmen waiting to take couples round Central Park in an open carriage for a dollar. In the daytime there was skating on two lakes in the Park and rambles among granite rocks and young birches, where one could easily imagine the Red Indians crouching, one feather askew, ready to war-whoop.

Prohibition didn't interest me, as I never tasted a cocktail until I was well on into my twenties; work in the theatre forbade late nights, there was no time for anything much except rehearsing with very little relaxation, fresh air, or adventuring. But very soon the whole pattern of life was to change.

That summer, there was an all-star production of *Becky Sharp* – great fun. It was the play that Minnie Maddern Fiske had played years before; she came one night, heavily veiled, and sat in the balcony and wrote me a lovely letter about Becky.

A spate of plays followed – most notably *Children of Darkness* by Edwin Justin Mayer which opened at the Biltmore in January 1930. It was about a group of people in Newgate Prison in the eighteenth century and was a great success. I played the Jailer's wench, and enjoyed every rollicking, bawdy romantic moment of it. The producer, Joseph Verner Reed, was a beginner in the theatre at that time and, despite his enthusiastic letters during the production, a couple of years later he wrote a very hurtful book about it, as well as about his other experiences in the theatre. His exposure of back-stage worries and stresses during the rehearsals was rather like a doctor or a priest betraying confidence; it is an unspoken rule among players that the result is what matters. Different temperaments react differently while people are trying their best for the good of the production and I think Mr Reed did not really know or like actors. I dislike 'star' behaviour for publicity or ego's sake, but Basil had fought for the best in the play and in despair one day he told me the only way we would get Reed to alter a certain scene would be for me to 'throw a temperament'. We were in Washington, trying out the play before the New York opening, so one night in the dressing-room I gave a performance specially for Mr Reed; I cried, stormed, and followed the plan Basil had suggested. The scene was changed, to the great benefit of the play, but Mr Reed never knew how or why – he only thought I was a bad-tempered actress, and followed this up years later with his book. I have Mr Reed's letters written during the working out of that fine play, insisting on his devotion and admiration. He had a very odd way of showing it. I was advised to let the letters of praise and appreciation be published to show his Judas-gesture towards people who had worked for him, but thought better of it.

Before *Children of Darkness* Basil and I had gone to England to visit his parents in London. They lived in an old house in Gloucester Place. His father had been a provincial manager, and had toured the famous operetta *Les Cloches de Corneville* all over the country; his mother, still very feminine and delicate, had played Lady Teazle and other heroines on tour. Basil, or Michael as his parents called him (how much nicer to be Michael), had literally been born in the theatre and had only had his parents to teach him. He had sat in front at rehearsals and in the wings at performances all through his childhood. He had a bad stammer when he was a boy and cured it by being made to recite Shakespeare over and over, day after day.

His parents' house looked like the antique booths at Portobello Market. I'm sure thousands of pounds worth of lovely things were gathering dust in those high ceilinged, damp rooms. His mother was like a magpie and later, when I returned to London to stay with them for a few months, she showed me boxes filled with fans and laces and stage trinkets she had collected. I was slightly shocked at the whole set-up. Basil had not seen his parents for years and, since he hardly ever wrote a letter, they were miles apart in every possible way. They felt he had wanted to forget them. I don't think this was so; it was only that it got more and more difficult to break the barrier of his guilt at seeming to neglect them. A sad business.

During that strange summer we discovered Étretat. We decided to go down to Devonshire for two weeks where it poured incessantly; so we crossed the Channel to the Normandy coast and followed our noses. They led us to Étretat, the most enchanting place to see and be in; a rocky coastline full of caves and arches, fisherman's lobster baskets, shrimping at low tide and on Sundays a stream of slow, black-clad peasants climbing up a green hill to a tiny white church. The hotel was a very nineteenth-century square white pension, 'Hôtel Blanquet', where the fishermen's boats lay upside down each night on the shingle beach next to great barrels of green disinfectant for their nets. One day I got so exasperated with *Lady Chatterley's Lover*, which I felt I should read, that I hurled it from the window into one of those vats – where no doubt an astonished fisherman found it later, suitably disinfected.

Walking through the cobbled side-streets of Étretat one morning, the sound of harp-music echoed into the sunlit silence. It was a strange sound to punctuate the early housewifely noises – scrubbing brushes, coffee-grinders and babies screaming. But later, on the beach, we saw someone looking like a young Russian spy, in a grey business suit, a slouch hat, very much out of the summer picture, kicking the pebbles at the sea's edge. It was Harpo. He came whenever he could, he said, to study with a teacher who lived in that remote French sea-side village. It makes the memory glow.

It was a heavenly interlude; long walks and bathing in the roughish sea, so that one came out with little blue bruises all over from the stirred-up shingle in the waves. A travelling circus came to town one day and the white horses stampeded on the evening we were there and frightened everyone so much that they fled from the tent, and the circus closed for lack of funds. The French have never known how to train animals. And at the Casino – a very small old-fashioned casino with two roulette tables – we gambled the outrageous sum of five francs each evening.

I went back to Étretat after the war to see what had happened – the whole place had been demolished in the Normandy landings. The Blanquet, the Casino, all gone – only by the enduring cliffs and the little chapel could I tell it was the place I had known and loved. A solitary fisherman's boat on the shingle had been made into a little kiosk and bore a plaque telling of the gallant dead. So many painters have immortalised its rocks and green-swards; but one's own memories of the laughter and simplicity of its folk are as sharp and sweet still, as that first taste of its local Calvados sipped through a lump of sugar.

Back in London we met Ashley Dukes. Basil had known him before and we had had correspondence about doing his play *The Man with a Load of Mischief* in New York. Mrs Dukes, now Dame Marie Rambert, was welcoming, and their house in Campden Hill was a lovely place to visit. The Ballet Rambert had started at the Mercury Theatre and I'm very proud to have known it in the beginning.

H.M. Harwood, the author, and Tennyson Jesse – 'Fryn' to her friends – had seen *Children of Darkness* in New York, and decided to bring it to London. The name of the play was changed – I don't know why – to *Knave and Quean*. Quean had to be explained as it was ye olde English for whore. This title put an entirely wrong emphasis on the play. We opened at the Ambassador's Theatre and were an immediate failure – all the more depressing because of its success in New York. It is interesting to note that the young poet was played by Robert Donat in London, I think his first London appearance. How beautiful he was.

Hopefully for me, the critics liked me so I felt I could, and would, come back. Basil took it badly as it was his return to his native London; so much so that at a supper party given for us at the Ritz he fainted dead away – from misery and, I think, too much drink.

There followed a barren period. We stayed with Basil's parents; I cooked our meals on an electric ring in one room. Basil left each day to renew theatre contacts; I felt I had to be patient as the failure of the play had been such a terrible disappointment to him. The months passed; I was offered plays but would not take anything until Basil found work. I knew his nature wouldn't tolerate my working before he did. This situation grew worse and worse. Basil's father was subject to fainting fits and therefore was not supposed to go out alone. But he did, several times, and I always had to go and claim him in the Paddington hospital. It was awful to see the straw-strewn cell-like cubicles where vagrants were huddled; and I was terribly ashamed when I felt the cold stare of the matron when I called for him. I loved the old man and there was no one else to come to his rescue. Basil would be out all day and his mother was too frail. It all became too much for me. I was afraid to go out and was given Luminal tablets by a doctor who looked like Mephistopheles.

Golding Bright, an endearing white-haired eccentric, saved my self-respect. He was the literary agent for J.M. Barrie and Somerset Maugham, among others, and was determined that I should have a success in London. He sent flowers, letters, took me to lunch, to theatres, introduced me to everyone. His wife was just as kind to me; she was an extraordinary woman who spoke seven languages, looked like Queen Alexandra, and wrote many books under the name of George Egerton. They lived in a flat near the British Museum and were everything I had imagined the Bloomsbury Edwardian intelligentsia should be. I owe my survival in those months to these two inimitable people. Golding arranged with Stuart Watson at the Haymarket for me to play in a comedy, *Queer Cattle* despite Basil's displeasure. The cast included Irene Vanbrugh, Ellis Jeffreys, Ian Hunter, Barry Jones, and myself.

I felt I was alive again. After it closed, Basil and I sailed back to New York, unknowingly into the best that was to come for us – The Theatre Guild and O'Neill's *Strange Interlude*.

The Theatre Guild was the most important theatrical organisation in New York. A beautiful new theatre had been built to house their productions. Every actor wanted above all things to work for them somehow, sometime. Lee Simonson was their resident scene-designer and one of the directors, and Basil and I had been filling their old abode, the Garrick Theatre, with our plays. The first time I had seen a Theatre Guild play was in that same Garrick Theatre in 1922: *He Who Gets Slapped* by Andreyev. My friend Romney Brent was playing a circus clown and I had gone backstage where he had introduced me to Basil, then one of the Guild's leading actors. I had known all the directors since those days in Greenwich Village before any of us had achieved or accomplished anything, when we took ourselves very seriously, and art was spelt with a capital 'A'. So, it was exciting to be asked by the Guild to take Eugene O'Neill's *Strange Interlude* to London. The fabulous Lunts, Alfred and Lynn, had been for years the established first players of the Guild, and indeed of the United States. Play after splendid play, year after year – they were the most respected and envied of actors. Miss Fontanne had been the original Nina in *Strange Interlude*; Judith Anderson had toured with it in the States – so I was thrilled to be chosen for the English adventure.

Everyone concerned was apprehensive about London's acceptance of this great play and perhaps they were readier to sacrifice me, if necessary, than the treasured Lunts. I realised this and was doubly determined to make a big success of it all. In those days, even though Sigmund Freud was widely read and discussed, Eugene O'Neill's concept of a woman's life and secret thoughts seemed very daring. I would have given anything to talk to O'Neill but had to be content with meeting his very beautiful wife and getting his blessing from her.

Owing to the technique of the play, and its double levels of
speech and thought, it had to be five-and-a-half hours long;
starting at five, breaking at eight to allow a dinner-hour; back
again from nine to eleven-thirty. We were all terrified lest
the conservative London audience would walk out at eight
o'clock and never come back, or come at nine, having missed
half the play. Every play since then has seemed an easy one to
learn – even *Mourning Becomes Electra* by the same author.

I can't remember much about the boat-trip over to England. We had had two weeks of playing at an uptown New
York theatre before embarking, and the company rehearsed
all the way over every day – we had to, in order to keep the
lengthy scenes co-ordinated – getting to know each other's
reactions more and more; it was the kind of play that did not
rely on an audience response; it just had to be done to its real
and deep values as though it were a very secret life that the
audience was being allowed to see. A kind of intellectual
voyeurism.

Basil and I took a small house in Park Village West, within
sound of the lions roaring in Regent's Park Zoo – and finally
on February 3rd 1931 the great day-night première happened
at the Lyric Theatre. It started at five-thirty. All I can say now
is that it was marvellous from the first. The Press went wild;
the audiences, struck dumb at the beginning, succumbed to
the unusual. Some went home at night in a daze to change into
evening clothes – sticking to tradition no matter what; others
came straight from work and ate their sandwiches in the
interval; some appeared in evening dress off the buses at five
o'clock and found restaurants that served special dinners so
that they could return in time to be in at the finish. Quotes
from the scenes crept into London conversation, and the very
ahead-of-the-times discussions of conception and pregnancy
and impotence and platonic love, and every phase of a
woman's impulses – and men's too – were madly disputed and
people came more than once: magazines, interviews, enthu-

siasm, arguments, the whole lot. Half a century on, I have re-read my most precious letter, from a very young Peggy Ashcroft, written immediately after she had seen the play:

> When I asked on Sunday night if I might come round and see you at the end of the play I didn't know what it was going to be like seeing 'Strange Interlude'. Now I do! I didn't not come round because I thought you would be tired – though you must be – but because first of all I could never have said one small part of how I enjoyed (a queer word!) your acting and your play. And I had that feeling which I think is rare, I don't ever remember feeling it before, that I couldn't bear to break the illusion – simply because for once the illusion had so completely taken me in and I believed you were Nina, and Ned and Charlie. Also – I had a very red nose!
>
> If all this sounds exaggerated and a little ridiculous you must blame yourself for acting me out of my senses. I have never loved the theatre so much as I did tonight. Thank you, thank you, both, *very* much – *and* Eugene O'Neill.

I wonder if, had there not been Eugene O'Neill, Hellman and Albee would have found themselves? It is startling to think how much is owed sometimes by one great writer to another, even perhaps to a lesser genius. The creative world feeds upon itself. On whom did Peter Shaffer feed to find the splendour of *Equus* and *Amadeus*? The chain is endless; one can see it in painting, hear it in music but nowhere is it as compelling as in the written word. It is a world of continual discovery, but it needs time and solitude – commodities hard to come by in 1982.

The success of *Strange Interlude* would have been fulfilling if Basil and my marriage had had any human reasonableness. All the rules had been laid down by Basil. He loved dogs and I love cats – so we bought a dog. A white West-Highland terrier, Midge, a great canine personality. He growled as every echo of the lions at the Zoo reached our little house and guarded us within an inch of his and our lives. He understood our strange hours, sleeping while we were at the theatre and ready for anything at midnight, when we returned wearily to drink Ovaltine or hot soup. Of course there were occasions when we had to pretend to lead glamorous actors' lives and be present at after-theatre parties, no matter how tired we were. But, even then, Midge would greet us, whatever the hour, with undying interest and vitality, knowing that about mid-day there would be a walk in Regent's Park and, from a distance, a look at the animals in the Zoo, body a-quiver, black nose twitching, slightly afraid, but game for a fight if necessary.

One day during this period we went to visit A.A. Milne in the country. Christopher Robin waved to us from a top dormer window when we left. I felt so vastly sorry for him, ridiculous I'm sure because his parents loved him very much. But he seemed such a lonely little boy. The garden was lovely, and Mrs Milne had beautiful red hair which made her look like a painting by Rossetti.

During the run of *Strange Interlude* we decided we would live in England. The theatre seemed so much more part of life here than in New York and, after all, it was Basil's home. So when the play ended I did not argue the point when he decided we should go back to New York; arrange to give up our flat there and say goodbye to our friends; when one is young and loving enough one does not question where work and life should be – it is enough that they just are. We took Midge along and when, after disposing of our New York flat, we went back to London we left him with a friend in the country.

Our next London abode was in Bruton Mews, off Berkeley Square, a strange little mews house with, of all things, a squash court, where the stable had been originally. Owen Nares wanted me for a play called *Double Harness* by an American, Edward Poor Montgomery. He was most understanding when I said I could not go to work before Basil got a job and told me he would hold the play for me – which he did, until Basil was asked to play in *Dinner at Eight*. I was thrilled

then to go right into rehearsal at the Haymarket – still my
favourite London theatre after Drury Lane. They both bear
their histories like an exquisite patina – no matter what non-
sense is housed in them sometimes – nothing can take away
the nobility; their walls and their stages remain proud and
tranquil.

Double Harness was one of those comedy-dramas of upper-
class domesticity so popular in the early thirties, complete
with mistress, wife, friend, dinner party, happy ending,
including a splendidly under-written scene between wife and
mistress at odds over the very attractive husband. Owen
Nares was a much better actor than he was given credit
for, since his extreme good looks had enlisted him into the
matinée-idol class. He was a most agreeable, highly professional actor-manager and his wife Marie sat in the stalls all
through rehearsals, keeping her eagle-jealous eyes on everyone and everything. At eleven o'clock Mr Nares had his
egg-nogg, and rehearsals broke promptly at five. We had had
difficulty casting someone for my younger sister. One day, a
slim girl with red-gold hair read the part – it was Iris Ashley
who later became the columnist and fashion writer of her day.
But even though she was unsure of herself then, she played the
part beautifully. It all seemed so relaxed and easy after the
O'Neill saga.

Owen Nares came and played squash at our mews house
sometimes and was consistently charming, but he could not
finish the run of the play – whether he was too ill or too tired, I
do not know. His leaving the cast was the cause of a most
extraordinary experience. I had heard of Henry Ainley, but
had never had the good fortune to see him on the stage, or to
hear his golden voice. It seems, for various reasons, he had not
been acting for some time. Mr Nares persuaded him to take
over his part in *Double Harness* as a come-back. So for three
weeks he rehearsed with us every day. He was still very
handsome, in a rather ravaged way; his voice like deep music,

THE GENTLE ART

OF MAKING LOVE.

These photographs of MR. OWEN NARES and MISS MARY ELLIS show them as they appear in " DOUBLE HARNESS," the successful comedy by Edward Poor Montgomery, which has just been transferred from the Haymarket to the Apollo. Mr. Owen Nares plays John Rockingham, the rising young barrister and potential Cabinet Minister, and Miss Mary Ellis is Sybil Livingstone, first his well-beloved mistress and then his not-so-well-beloved wife.

26 With Owen Nares in *Double Harness*, 1933

27 As Frieda Hatzfield in Jerome Kern's *Music in the Air*,
His Majesty's Theatre, London, 1933

28 With my dresser, Maudie Farace, Hollywood, 1935

his performance strong and touching, and his presence in the play would have brought everyone to see it again. Then on the dress-rehearsal day he disappeared. The publicity had been terrific – naturally, for Ainley to be returning, it would be. But he was nowhere to be found. They finally tracked him down; the demon had taken full possession again. When I saw him and asked him why, why, why? he wept and said at the last moment he could not face critics and audiences again, but had managed until the final rehearsal to keep his courage up. My heart ached for him, because of him; and somehow the fact that the play had to go on with a competent understudy, and on tour also, seemed unimportant. I felt I had been working with an Olympian for weeks and had been touched by his magic. My regret for him, and appreciation of him, will never leave me.

Basil was happy in his play. He complained continually about a young actress in it – in the light of subsequent events it was somewhat ironical. I should have known it was to blind me to what was happening; but it never occurred to me then that anyone could take such great pains to hide and plan and connive. I had been hoping that life would become simple and uncomplicated. There was theatre, there was love. One could fail and survive in either of them.

During the play at the Haymarket, C.B. Cochran had summoned me to his Bond Street office. He lectured me on the folly of not singing any more . . . it had been ten years since *Rose Marie* and since then my career in New York and London had been built only in the 'legitimate' theatre. That word is so peculiar in that context – as though singing in opera, or a musical play was an illegal, punishable offence. Indeed, C.B. thought it time I should be punished. He had a play, with music by Jerome Kern and Oscar Hammerstein II, called *Music in the Air*, which he planned to put on at His Majesty's. He was very persuasive – besides being his practical, intelligent and likeable self – and I found myself accepting the idea happily. He promised me one thing; London audiences didn't know I could sing, and he and I agreed not to mention the fact until they had heard and seen me for themselves in the play; so, as far as London knew, I was just to follow *Double Harness* with another play that 'had some music'. I hired a piano which could hardly be fitted into the little mews house and learned the score as quietly as possible, so as not to disturb the neighbours around Berkeley Square where nightingales had been known to sing. I had not sung for eight years, so I put myself on a training course. When I had left *Rose Marie* in 1925, Desirée Ellinger had taken over. An odd coincidence was that when I came to London, I learned that the famous throat specialist Geoffrey Carte was her husband; and odder still, years later, to find that her daughter was my understudy in *Arc de Triomphe*. Basil seemed glad about it all and the days flew into production of one of the loveliest of musical plays; everyone was happy, Cochran delighted and I was on the verge of another of those somersaulting changes in my life, events I could never have foreseen.

Music in the Air was a joyful thing. The morning after we opened, Mr Cochran telephoned and asked me to come to the front of house entrance instead of the stage door, when I reached the theatre for the evening performance. I got there at about seven – and almost fainted. Every poster, sign, and the great lights over the theatre just said MARY ELLIS IN MUSIC IN THE AIR. This was his way of saying thank you and making me know that London had liked me. The critics behaved as though it was a miracle that I could sing – and I was 'discovered' as a singer; but suddenly they connected up the opera and *Rose Marie* and wouldn't let it go. From then on it was a fight to persist as a non-singing actress, and I continually had to explain myself. I felt exactly as I had always done; I've never been able to realise it's me – up there in lights, or on a bill-board, or in photographs, or in the newspapers. It was all hard to take, every time. It always seemed to be happening to

someone else; and now, when I write about it, I am completely removed and self-critical, and sometimes angry. I have
been fortunate in that, in the main, critics have liked my
work; and I am grateful to the ones that offered constructive
criticism – I've always noted and remembered the bad reviews
more than the good ones. The ego always suffers – one grows
more and more vulnerable, not less so – and it is a hurtful
experience always, having done one's best, in good faith, to be
put down. But this happens to all individuals and workers in
every field. For the painter, the writer, it is easier, I think,
because it is not such a personal thing; on the stage one's *person*
is sometimes attacked; it can be healthy and helpful when it is a
corrective – but can also be destructive, to the point of despair.

Music in the Air was a perfect professional experience; but
my personal life was to have its worst upset. We had moved
to a house on the edge of Regent's Park, taking with us
our lovely cat and Mrs Gwen Bocking, a comfortable cook-
housekeeper, who had come to us in Bruton Mews. We had
many visitors. Mabel Terry-Lewis came to lunch one day,
with her two black spaniels – one of them had hysterics and
had to be covered up with a table-cloth; my cat rushed down
to the cellar and wouldn't come out for days! We had been to
her lovely country house for tea one Sunday, where I met John
Gielgud for the first time – slim, aloof, beautiful, standing
quietly in corners, looking just like Hamlet, of course. I was
too shy to talk to him.

Trying not to believe rumours and what I instinctively
knew was happening, my distress made me lose my voice for
a week. Finally, at the end of his play *Dinner at Eight*, one
spring day, Basil left for New York. He looked very happy as
he stepped into a taxi in the sunshine, wearing a broad-
brimmed panama hat, carrying his ivory-headed walking
stick; I leaned out of the window in the early morning and we
waved goodbye to each other; and the next thing I heard was
that he was living in a New York hotel with that young actress

from *Dinner at Eight*. I'm sure he was much in love with her; they stayed together for years until he left her, too, and married another actress.

On that spring day in 1934 I blamed myself, again, as usual. I can never unlove someone I have loved, no matter what happens; this has somewhat overcrowded my emotional equipment, and in this case I hit a new low. I took Mrs Bocking and my cat and moved to a small house. *Music in the Air* went on and on.

I met and re-met lots of kindly people. Especially the Freres – Mrs Frere, the warm-hearted Pat Wallace, Edgar Wallace's daughter, was the first one to tell me years ago that I must write this book. At their parties everyone from Somerset Maugham to Nancy Spain gossiped; literary and theatrical barbed spikes, true or untrue. I met Maugham's nephew Robin and his niece Katemary Bruce, herself a novelist. It was a delight to go to her house after the theatre and meet her Edwardian mother who looked as though she should always wear a veil and a bunch of parma violets and ride in a hansom-cab; and Lord Maugham, her father, who liked singing old songs with me after we had supped on kippers and champagne – surely the most delectable combination possible.

At Katemary's house in Cadogan Square, the gatherings through the years were stimulating – it was there I was once startled by H.G. Wells' piping-high voice; and Rebecca West attracted and frightened me in equal measure; and of course 'Uncle Willy' Maugham, if he was in London, benignly cynical, looking more like a Chinese sage every year. Despite the stimulation of talk and personalities, I felt more and more alone.

Maudie Farace had come to be my dresser at this time and stayed with me for years. She was English to the core, her profession as dresser handed down from her mother; they both proudly said 'we of the theatre'. She had been a dancer and on a tour to Scandinavia had met her Italian musician husband; I saw him playing the piano-accordion once in Lyon's Corner House. Their daughter Eileen had to be given every advantage that they had never had, and later married someone high-up in the police force. Maudie made life backstage in the theatre comfortable and loving. It was she who never showed nerves or fluster, who knew what make-up to arrange, who kept costumes meticulously fresh, who boiled an egg for tea on matinée days, dimmed the light and covered me with a blanket to rest, kept unwanted visitors away, wept tears or laughed with me, and lived devotedly without sentimentality – indeed, scolding and criticising when necessary. She was of a breed no longer in the theatre and as much part of the success as any on-stage talent. We went through much together – even Hollywood – and there were many times when she cooked and cleaned and stayed with me and saved me from fright and loneliness in an arid theatrical desert.

The dressing-room at His Majesty's was a 'grand suite' – a salon, the dressing-room itself, and a big old-fashioned mahogany-trimmed bathroom. During the run of the play there were many guests and I felt like the story-book actresses. A Viscount sent red roses every week in a box that looked as if it were made of ruby-coloured suede; the then Prince of Wales came, and there was a party at the Café de Paris afterwards. People came again and again. Even Christopher Robin was there one matinée with his parents. He sat in the front row and was brought backstage afterwards. When I asked him if he had enjoyed himself he said 'I was sick'. I never discovered whether from excitement or distaste.

At one matinée at His Majesty's I noticed a young man almost leaning onto the stage from a box. That evening, lilies arrived at the theatre – enough to grace a funeral or fill three dressing-rooms – with a note signed 'Ivor Novello'. The name meant nothing to me except for 'Keep the Home Fires Burning'. I did not sense what was to come of that visit of his, but I remembered always that extraordinary face turned up to

me from the stage-box – lit by a reflection of the footlights.
There seemed to be no-one else in the theatre but him and me.

*   *   *

I decided it would be sensible to have a house in the country
where I could get away from everything at weekends. I drove
out of London for miles and miles on Sundays, following up
advertisements and going to country estate agents. Finally I
came upon 'Miswells'. It was a small eighteenth-century
house in Sussex with miles of uninterrupted views across
meadows and woodland. I leased it for an indefinite period of
years at a now ridiculous sum and furnished it with country
things (except Heal's beds, and a Bechstein piano). There was
only one bathroom, so I had basins put in the bedrooms and
had a modern kitchen installed; the 'piggeries' were made into
a playroom and I had a tennis court put down, and two French
windows made to lead into the garden. For sunny weekends
there were hammocks hung in the orchard – and there was tea
in the little rose-garden; thinking of it now, and the friends
who gathered there, it is like another world entirely.

Mrs Bocking, my cook, came too – and my cat, who
learned not to touch baby birds but sometimes brought me
half a rabbit as a great treat. Thereupon I had a grisly hour
looking for the other half in the garden, usually found in the
rain-barrel, or in a wheel-barrow, to the disgust and fury of
Mr Austen, the splendid Sussex gardener who lived in the
cottage. He grew all our vegetables and strawberries and apples
and the house was warm and comfortable: I can remember the
lovely smell of polished wood and fires and opening the
casement window in the early morning after a showery night
to the chorus of birds chattering and drying their feathers in
the sunshine. I like to believe no other country in the world
offers this particular magic.

The spell was broken when the Teddington Studios asked

me to do my first film *Bella Donna*. I had to leave at six every morning to be on the set at Teddington, made up and ready, at nine. That script of *Bella Donna* was terrible, but Conrad Veidt was in it, and Cedric Hardwicke. To work with Veidt was a lovely experience in itself; he was an outsize personality, very funny and angry by turns and terribly attractive. A pale, red-haired American, Robert Milton, was the director. He was of the theatre, and I don't think making films was his milieu. But we battled through and I've seen the film several times over the years (it's still in the Archives, I believe) and it is not much worse than most films of that time. At one point in the story I got led into the desert on a donkey (piles of sand on the studio floor – no voyaging in those days to Arabian desert locations) by a young Arab wearing a fez and a striped gown. The young Arab turned out to be one Rodney Millington, in a very dark-brown make-up, long before he became the head of *Spotlight* and known, I think, to every actor in the world.

Music in the Air was over, so I gave up the London house. All that had been *Music in the Air* vanished; but at least the gramophone records are there to remind me, and anyone else who wants to remember. It's a sad fact of the theatre: all the work, the companionship and constant daily effort to please audiences, disappear as the final curtain comes down.

Then came an extravagant, over-dressed translation from the Hungarian, directed by an unknown Mittel-Europa ego-maniac; a Napoleonic semi-tragedy, *Josephine*. The only thing worth remembering about *that* production at His Majesty's was Emlyn Williams' adaptation and the fact that he stepped in at the last minute to play my son; otherwise it was bemused torture for all of us – fortunately for only ten days. A re-sounding, hilarious failure.

Then the call came from Paramount, offering a two-year contract to do three films for a great deal of money – in those days one could really save it, too! It meant leaving for Holly-wood in the autumn. I persuaded my dresser Maudie's family

to let her come with me to California; she wanted to very
much, so all was well.

The journey was arranged by Paramount; reservations fit
for a princess on a Cunarder, and at the Waldorf Astoria Hotel
in New York, before I boarded the train for Los Angeles. It
was of course how they treated all their 'stars', but to me it was
fabulous, and I was wildly excited; I tried my best not to show
it. At least I had learned a modicum of reserve in England; but
it was hard not to explode and hit the ceiling like a champagne
cork. One day as I was packing, the telephone rang: it was Ivor
Novello, asking if he could talk to me about a play with music
for Drury Lane. That great theatre had been having bad luck
for some years and the idea was to establish its importance
again by a very special production. Drury Lane was almost the
size of the Metropolitan Opera House, and the acoustics were
even better – so the idea was a temptation from the first. I
explained that I was just setting out for Hollywood for two
years, but Ivor said he must see me and settle everything
before I went away . . . he himself would manage to persuade
Paramount to let me come back in the Spring for King George
V's Silver Jubilee and the opening of Drury Lane . . . on and
on it went, the tempting insistence. I felt I had no way of
handling it, so I did what I still do, at stressful times – I relaxed
completely and let it happen if it could, and should. It evidently could, for it was all arranged by Ivor, the agents,
Paramount, and Drury Lane.

Before I left, Ivor outlined the story to me, which was very
much the King Carol-Lupesco romance, plus. He promised to
send the script and his recordings of the music as he wrote it,
day by day. I have all those first records, made at his flat, with
him playing as he composed; and Christopher Hassall's lyrics
came with them by post to Hollywood, every week.

There was too much on my plate. Finally, the day of sailing
came. Maudie and I embarked at Southampton and I had
seven days of rest in a regal stateroom suite, far above my

station, I felt, but it was easy to get used to it, and I enjoyed every moment.

New York was like an exquisite Martian city of glass and concrete towers. Every time I go back, I get a tonic thrill; but so much more in those days than now; when one sailed into the harbour, instead of flying over Long Island Sound, as that sky-line evolved out of a sun-lit mist, the visual surprise and beauty made one feel like an explorer.

The rooms on the thirty-sixth floor of the Waldorf Astoria hotel were awesome; black marble, thick pile carpet, bells and telephones galore. I felt pretty foolish, like a very small nut in a huge shell, when my parents and friends visited me there during the two-day stay before I boarded the train westward. I could never get used to the outsize grapefruit, giant-size prawns, iced everything and absolutely springing page-boy service that came two at a time, if one pressed a button. But this was in 1935, and all paid for by Paramount. When I visit New York now, it's a very different story. Maudie was over-whelmed by the whole thing; and I remember we stood at a window late at night, in our plain English dressing-gowns, looking westward and southward at the city, lights of every colour, fire engines, police, and ambulances wailing into the unresponsive air; six unknown mysterious months ahead of us.

3

Scene Changes

The train journey to Los Angeles took four days and three nights. Ginger Rogers and her mother were travelling in the next compartment. Every half-hour a white-coated black porter knocked to ask if we wanted anything – every meal, every stop, particularly as the train sped into the west, and past Indian reservations and cornfields, was an adventure. The vastness of the country was unbelievable to me, as I had been hemmed into New York and a few eastern cities during most of my childhood and ten years of theatre; the expanse of wheat-fields, and farms, and valleys and hills was endless, and made the end in view seem trivial; but the arrival at Los Angeles and all the arrangements for my welfare soon cancelled any feeling of uselessness, and I was keen to get to work. It took some weeks before I did. Camera tests, story conferences, photographs, interviews, all in a strange atmosphere, and almost a strange language.

The studio had reserved an apartment for me in the Chateau Marmont, a rather sordid-splendid place, where I found Constance Collier, and others I was to know, firmly established. A lot of invitations awaited me and besides all day at the studio, while the first film was being written, composed and got ready, I had the heady experience of meeting everyone who had been just a film name to me.

Jean Negulesco was scheduled to direct my first test. It was no less than a whole scene from Mascagni's *Cavalleria Rusticana*. He introduced me to Elissa Landi, who was a great friend of his. She took me under her wing and made me feel at home. She was one of the loveliest people I have ever known. Supposedly a descendant of Elizabeth of Austria (she looked very like her) she, her mother and her brother had an estate in the hills above Santa Monica. Avocados, orange-groves, grapefruit ready to be picked; the house filled with antique furniture; wide terraces and wonderful cooking: it even had an organ placed so one could play looking towards a gorgeous landscape and, at her open-house Sunday lunches, I met everyone; many old friends from the theatre in London – Hollywood seemed to be in a fever about British authors and actors. Elissa herself was beautiful and warm, intelligent and great fun. She never became a great star; but maybe, just because Hollywood never really 'got her', she remained a very special person.

Maudie took everything in her enthusiastic stride and kept house in our three-room flat, with its balcony facing the sun-rise. The studio had had a grand-piano installed and supplied a car and chauffeur. I was freshly unbelieving every morning when Maudie gave me breakfast at six on the balcony, where we watched the sun come up blood-red, before we were driven to the studios for the day's work; and I was too tired at the end of the day to go to any of the dinners or parties. Only Saturday evenings were possible, knowing I could sleep on Sunday, and rest, except for an hour or two of practising.

The most fascinating friend I made, introduced to me by Elissa, was Fritz Lang, the German director; he had escaped from Germany as the Nazis took over – they had burned his library, his manuscripts, and many of his films; his wife had joined the Hitler contingent – and when he reached England before coming to the United States, he unaccountably had not found work. The great films *Metropolis* and *M* and other less magnificent ones had found world audiences: even so Holly-wood was still trying to find a place for this great man; and since I spoke German, he would come in his rickety little car on days when I was free and we would drive out into the desert, to lakes rimmed with salt where everything their waters touched turned bone-white, and to the Mexican border, past monasteries, fishing-villages, and strange pink stone landscapes. For some reason he called me 'Monkey', but this was offset by the big box of tuberoses which came every Sunday morning. One weekend I stayed with him at his house. My breakfast tray brought in by a silent Chinese boy had a rose on it and a telegram saying 'Good morning, I hope you slept well'. And as I came downstairs later, a terrible electric piano was tinkling 'The Bells of St Mary's'. It was all at such odds with this sophisticated, erudite, complex personality. I can only think he lived, tongue-in-cheek, watching how certain behaviour affected his friends; or perhaps his genius demanded an almost suburban sentimentality sometimes, completely removed from his usual life-style. I never found out.

All was set for my first film *All The King's Horses* – a pretty mediocre effort, with perhaps some charm. Carl Brisson was the King of the title – in a white uniform, stretched as tight as possible over his somewhat plump behind – and singing a catchy song called 'A Little White Gardenia', as he flashed a dimpled smile. I had lots of fun playing his rebel Queen, who ran away to the Gypsies, from the stuffiness of the Ruritanian Court – until he shaved off his beard and won her back in a more human mood, still with a dimpled smile, and even tighter trousers. There were Gypsy songs, waltzes and everything one could wish for in the Kalman-Lehár-Straussian mould.

He introduced me to his overpowering, tall Danish wife, and to his brother who was, I was later told, really his son. But he wanted to stay young and dimpled, poor man!

The nicest thing that happened during *All The King's Horses* was that I was able to invite my mother and father to Hollywood; to put them up at the best hotel, to give them a big party, to have them on the set at the studio for the day, where they saw it all happening. I asked Father who he would like to sit next to at the party and he said Miriam Hopkins – so Miss Hopkins it was who partnered him. He looked so handsome, his greying Van Dyck beard, his goldrimmed glasses on a black cord – and of course, white tie and tails. Mother was in her element too, with the film-stars; it was a great joy to me to be able to give them this. Father made me buy a mink coat while they were there. I had no desire or intention to do so, but he had five sent to me on approval and I marched up and down in front of him for him to choose the one he wanted me to buy. I was determined to save all my money; he made me spend some of it, nevertheless expecting me to be thrifty, which owing to his initial teachings, I have been (and sometimes wish I hadn't). That coat lasted for years, and ended up as a lining in an overcoat for a very 'camp' acquaintance.

Before my second film started, I was allowed a short holiday. So I booked a bungalow at La Quinta, a desert hotel, full of flowers, and quiet as Death Valley. Grizelda Harvey came with me, and of course Maudie – and there was a week of bliss and nothingness except sunshine and longing for home and England.

Having got me over the baptism of the studios, Paramount really got down to it and started preparing a splendid film for me – Tullio Carminati and Ida Lupino were also in it; and Lewis Milestone, of *All Quiet on the Western Front* fame, was the director. It was called *Paris Love-Song* and working in it was one of the most enjoyable times I ever had.

All this time the records for *Glamorous Night* were arriving . . . and I was corresponding with Ivor about the script, the scenery, the costumes – the director.

More about that when the time comes. I am still on the set of *Paris Love Song*, as though it were yesterday. We worked in those days till midnight if necessary. I had one song in which I played three different characters and instead of breaking the sequence, as they expected, in order to change make-up and costume in a matter of hours, I asked for the quick changes to be done as they would have been in the theatre, in less than a minute. The stage crew and cameramen had never seen such a thing, so I was the heroine of the day; also I did all direct singing – no dubbing, no recording. At the end of the film we had a big party and I was really lifted on high in the slinky black sequinned dress of the cabaret scene. Every day in the making of that film had been hours and hours of hard work and interest and fun. Milestone was a very Russian-American personality – full of humour and imagination; I adored him; Carminati, delightful; Ida Lupino very young and very good. One day the telephone rang on the set for me; I hated this kind of interruption, so was rather cross when I answered it – it was Leopold Stokowski, my Archangel of the Alps, asking if I could get him into the studios; he said he was determined to break into the film world. Naturally I couldn't help him myself – but I reported it to the 'high-ups', and ultimately I'm sure Stokowski got what he wanted. In the following year I was to have a really strange meeting with him.

I did not see much of Hollywood, and what I did see of it seemed to me a rather sad, dirty place, outside the bustle and business-like atmosphere of the studios. The few homes I visted were very much as any country houses anywhere: there was more sunshine, many swimming pools and plenty of Chinese and Polynesian houseboys and butlers, but the few stars I knew were very conventional and hard-working and because I didn't really belong there, perhaps everybody was on their good behaviour. Anyway, there was no time to discover or analyse anything.

I was not a great party-goer, so never saw the legendary drinking and carousing I'd heard about, and I don't believe it existed; not at any rate among the people I met and not any worse I'm sure than anywhere else in the world. Young people came there, determined to get into that sham world and ready with a sort of dreadful heroism to experience anything or anybody. There was an undercurrent of desperation in the dusty air and an uncaring atmosphere; but I felt this only when I was driven along the brassy streets or went shopping – never in the studios where the routine was ruthless and patience a necessary virtue.

There were Sundays when I didn't have to film that were days of homesickness. Maudie would cook a chicken or a piece of beef with all the trimmings and we would eat it on the balcony, wondering how the weather was in England. After months of dry, sunny days, the thought of pale blue cloud-tufted skies, even the hushing fogs, the light snows, the biting cold, the early evening golden-lit streets – all seemed very important. It was March, and very hot already in California. I had been thrilled by a lot, and disgusted by a little. I had seen Mae West on the set, bare to the hips, having her plaster corset sandpapered into that perfect hour-glass shape, an enormous black-feathered hat on her head, giving directions to several attending henchmen; I had been happy to know Marlene Dietrich's dressing-room was opposite mine at the studios (the dressing-rooms were like beautiful little country bungalows): it was lovely to talk to her, in the early morning before she had any make-up on her face. When I first came she sent me yellow roses – when I left there were masses of sweet-peas in my cabin on the boat: but perhaps this was because I had become a friend of Fritz Lang's. I had taken Lord Byng of Vymy to lunch in the canteen, when he came to visit the studios; I had watched a very stout and ageing Mrs Patrick Campbell receiving guests at Charles Boyer's party, as though she were the hostess. I had been taken to the big gambling club and watched a white-faced star lose a fortune and had had supper at a one-room Russian restaurant where I watched the host cook a real Boeuf Strogonoff. Fritz had taken me to eat Chinese food in sleazy downtown Los

Angeles; to the Brown Derby, where resting film actors went to lunch (if they could afford it) hoping to catch the searching eye of some producer; to a Fish-Special in San Diego. I had watched a very young Bette Davis buying shoes in Magnin's Department Store and Gloria Swanson had invited me to lunch. And all I wanted was to wake up in Sussex, with my Persian cat purring on the windowsill.

On the boat on the way home, I learned the script of *Glamorous Night*, knowing the whole company would have been at it already for ten days. When I arrived I felt as though I were coming out of an anaesthetic – gradually, on the boat, people had become people again; the sea was real salt-water, food tasted like food, and the north-country stewardess called me 'luv'. Maudie started getting a light behind her eyes as we neared the white cliffs and the screaming gulls were a fanfare of welcome. But I wasn't prepared for Victoria Station; Ivor was there, with the director, Leontine Sagan, to rush me off to Drury Lane where the whole cast and management were assembled in the upstairs bar, waiting, with champagne. Lyn Harding, Barry Jones, Trefor Jones, Olive Gilbert, Peter Graves, Elizabeth Welch, and what seemed like hundreds of singers and dancers and musicians – I could feel their suspicious, questioning good-will, and it made me doubly anxious to be everything they expected of me.

*　　　*　　　*

It is impossible to translate the quality of a person into words; they sound bleak compared with the blaze, the excitement and the enthusiasm which Ivor created. He had complete faith in himself and what he was doing and in the people he had chosen to do it with him. Because of this, everyone felt bound to do their utmost for him. His reward was the response from the packed houses, loyalty, devotion. My friendship with him lasted until his death. It delights me to write about him. Despite his huge success, he remained unspoiled. His mis-

29 & 30 The Paramount film *All the King's Horses*: myself in a typical Hollywood setting of the 1930s and with Carl Brisson

31 With Lord Byng of Vimy and Carl Brisson in the studio canteen, Hollywood, 1935

32 At the Paramount Studios during the making of *Paris Love Song*, 1935, with left to right, Ida Lupino, Tullio Carminati, Lewis Milestone, the director and James Blakeley

chievous grin, his acceptance of criticism, his unstinting praise of things that pleased him, counteracted any flaws in his personality. Highly emotional, non-intellectual, he had read everything, seen everything. There was, of course, the unsure, hidden facet of him which I was to see quite often. Neither his gaiety nor his depressions were those of the true sophisticate. Had he lived beyond his fifty-eight years, there is no telling how good his music might have become. There was danger in his facility; he used to say 'I have run dry', but before an hour had passed he could whirl into a whole new plot and score – with breathless activity. Not always very good, either. He sometimes wrote the most awful 'kitsch'; but he knew this, he almost did it on purpose. On the other hand, when during the war he composed an act of an opera *Joan of Arc* for me, in *Arc de Triomphe*, James Agate, our doyen-critic, wrote that he should now go ahead and write the whole opera. But in 1935 *Glamorous Night* was enough. It put Drury Lane back into its destined greatness as a theatre. The real satisfaction I had was that he often said I stimulated him to new thoughts, new things, new music. My regret now is that I did not worry him enough into constant composing. In *Glamorous Night* he was careful in his music and musicianly – he was conscious of orchestration always and could have scored everything himself.

During the weekends at his country house, Redroofs, he and I would lie on his over-long sofa, feet to feet, listening to everything: Schönberg, Strauss, Ravel, Mahler, and of course all the older classics. But he got just as much enjoyment from performances in the lightest field – I've never known such a wide-spread appreciation of the best in every form of entertainment. When Flagstad came to London, we went to her rehearsals at Covent Garden – I often sat next to him at these – and I believe that whatever he felt he lacked in himself, he worshipped in others. He went to every play, every opera, every film. Besides all this professionalism, he was able to love deeply, advise wisely; and fight like a stubborn tiger for what he believed in – sometimes to his own misfortune.

Oliver Messel's genius for settings and costumes helped to create the magic of *Glamorous Night* – a shipwreck, a pillared palace, a Gypsy encampment and a baroque stage within a stage – all this I am sure wove the spell, just as Christopher Hassall's lyrics made the songs seem like poetry. Ivor had had immense foresight – the secondary plot dealt with the use of television in recording foreign events and this, in 1935, was certainly seeing into the future, also the story had an unhappy ending – not the easy solution that usually brings the curtain down on an operetta.

We worked late into the night for five weeks, Sagan, Ivor and myself. Sagan rehearsed relentlessly. She had directed *Children in Uniform* and she bullied and scolded. I could not imagine why Ivor had chosen her until I met her and endured her; that is the only word I can use. She was a tyrant, but she got results so it was worth it and we accepted it gratefully. I burst into tears during one rehearsal, unable to stand the strain, whereupon her voice shouted from the stalls in a sharp, German accent: '*Now* you must sing, that is what I want you to be, hysterical and furious and weeping!' Suddenly to have to sing on top of this was almost impossible but somehow I managed to do it and to repeat it at every performance was a new technical experience.

Trevor Jones was a fine Welsh tenor, a dear little round man exactly like the opera-singer he had to play; Lyn Harding a threatening villain; Barry Jones the king I had to marry and Ivor, of course, the young Englishman who had come to this court to establish television and fallen for the Mistress-Queen of the country. Oh dear, how like all the Transylvanian plots it sounds, but somehow it wasn't like them and the opening night was something I shall never forget – nor, I am sure will any of those who were fortunate enough to be there.

Ivor gave me a small diamond and ruby cross on a golden

chain for the first night. It became a barometer of moods for the cast. When I did not wear it they knew Ivor and I were angry with each other and they were especially nice to us. It happened very seldom.

There was a tragi-comic incident one evening. In a scene where I led the revolutionary 'people' to the King's Palace, Ivor had to shoot at the villain, Lyn Harding. The stage shot went wild and peppered Lynn's bottom, but he took it in his stride, literally, and all was well.

The Jubilee of King George V and Queen Mary was celebrated during our opening week. Ivor and I hung out of the windows of his Aldwych flat and managed to catch sight of the royal coach and the crowds, and that weekend I went to his house in the country where his mother, Madame Clara Novello-Davies, dressed in a green velvet house-gown, stood up *every* time the National Anthem was played on the radio, which was about every ten minutes, and toasted it in brandy. She finally had to remain seated.

That year, George V, Queen Mary, and the Duke and Duchess of Kent came to Drury Lane; it was the last play George V came to and we all felt very proud. Queen Mary was a keen theatre-goer. In subsequent years, whenever she graced the Royal Box in theatres where I played, I was always thrilled to make my curtsy and talk to her; she offered such astute criticism and appreciation, and was gracious without condescension – truly royal.

The first night party had been terrific. Noel Coward spent a lot of time telling Ivor what he thought of the play and where it should be changed – but Ivor, riding on the wave of a great success, smiled patiently and wouldn't have changed anything for the world – he didn't need to. I think Coward and Ivor had a professional love-hate relationship all their lives; mutual admiration for totally different gifts. Ivor's musical plays were always sold out for weeks before they opened and he fed that theatre public of the thirties with an uncomplicated delight.

The weekends in Sussex were something to look forward to – friends, and music, and walks: Christopher Hassall came often and wrote some of his best poems there. On the cover of his first edition of a collection of them he wrote, for my birthday: 'For Mary, in gratitude because she makes his lyrics sound like real poetry! With love, Christopher, June 15th 1935'. Peter Graves came often, too, only twenty-one, tall, very British, and full of fun.

I have kept that guest-book of those weekends, and it reads like pages from *Who's Who*. Even Ivor broke his vow never to 'go visiting' and came down. Sometimes John McCormack and Lily would drive down in their huge white car. They came to Drury Lane more than once and we discovered that John and I had the same birth date (though not the same number of years); so at midnight June 15th–16th we went to the Savoy for a late supper to celebrate. We sang at some of the same galas that season, and I remember standing in the wings waiting for my turn at the Marie Tempest jubilee concert, listening to McCormack sing 'Where e'er you Walk'; and as an encore 'Snowy Breasted Pearl', and feeling I had no business to dare to sing after that.

Mother and Father came over in the summer and Father's entrance into my dressing-room after the performance was my reward for years of hard work. He was beaming and just said 'Wonderful – wonderful', with tears in his eyes. My mother's only comment was that one of my costumes was unbecoming. A double pleasure for my parents – and me – was that *Paris Love Song*, the film with Carminati, was running in London at the same time as *Glamorous Night* and there were giant posters everywhere. It was splendid, too, that Mother and Father were able to visit me in the country. They both loved the house and Father played the country-squire for several weeks. It was gorgeous June weather, undisturbed save for the vague Hitler rumbles and the bleak prospect of having to go back to Hollywood to finish my contract whenever *Glamorous Night* ended. There were special charity performances; meetings with greats and ingrates; having fun coming out of the stage-door; looking small and plain, and telling the waiting crowd 'Miss Ellis left by the front of house half an hour ago.' I still have a passion for anonymity.

The working relationship with Ivor developed into a very good kind of loving. To my mother it was incomprehensible that it did not entail a romantic ending: I tried to explain it all to her, but she would have none of it.

That golden summer sped into a copper autumn. Then the blow fell. The theatre was packed out week after week – there were bookings into the New Year – there was every reason to think that there would be a very long run, but, unknown to Ivor and all of us, the Drury Lane management, not knowing that *Glamorous Night* would change the fortunes of the theatre and be a huge success, had chosen to play safe and before it opened had committed the theatre to the usual pantomime at Christmas. We were stunned. Everything was done to try to prevent this happening, but they had firmly contracted the Christmas pantomime and there was nothing to be done but close a magnificent success before Christmas. It must have been one of the most ridiculous and tragic things to happen in the theatre – unbelievable. Ivor took it very well, considering. And I had to go back to Hollywood as I had promised, for the third film.

During the summer I had become very friendly with Tim Brooke. He had stood in the wings at Drury Lane often and had come for most weekends. If Chris Hassall was there also, we would put on César Franck's Symphony on Sunday mornings to start the day; and when Romney came for a long visit the house would be full of the sounds of Brahms, Wagner and Strauss. Tim had already written three successful novels – *Man Made Angry*, *Miss Mitchell* and *Saturday Island*. Born Hugo von Böhr, his family had changed the name to Brooke in the First World War. His father was Clifford Brooke, the theatre director, working in New York; his mother, a religious fanatic, living the life of a nun. Tim seemed a very introvert young man. A few years younger than I was, he was an enchanting companion, full of humour and imagination. He would say to me 'I feel safe with you'. I never knew quite how to take this, but I knew he was lonely and I was pleased when he decided to come to Hollywood after Christmas to see me.

I thought it was extravagant to keep the country house going, with gardener and Mrs Bocking, while I was away for six months again so I arranged to cancel my lease. The dogs and cats I gave to Mr Austen, the gardener, and Mrs Bocking tearfully decided to retire. I was very sad about it all and the gate shut on a very happy house.

Maudie could not come with me this time, so a strange woman, secretary-cum-hairdresser-cum-general factotum accompanied me; she remained in Hollywood after I left and I believe became some sort of agent. On my way there, in New York this time at a much more modest hotel, Maria Ouspenskaya came to see me; she looked much older, but was her usual exuberant self and seemed content. I did not have time to see many people, but I had for a long time wanted to find out what had happened to Susan Sayre Titsworth (that name again!), my English teacher at school. I traced her to a convent where she was still teaching; we had a wonderful meeting and I was glad to be able to tell her how much she had helped me long ago. To her I was still the little girl who had adored her and won school prizes for composition. She still expected me to be a writer and tried to overlook the fact that I had gone into the theatre – she had expected better things of me.

When I arrived in Hollywood just before Christmas, again at the seedy Chateau Marmont, Fritz Lang had presents waiting – a long-playing record of Stephen Foster's songs and a Mexican Madonna made of one piece of cedar wood. She is in some corner wherever I live.

The first thing to be done in my second Hollywood season was to find a house for a few months. I was lucky, and found a small Beach House at Santa Monica. It had belonged to Norma Talmadge and had a salt-water pool built on its terrace above the Pacific; the bedrooms looked for miles out to sea, and there were two people who came with the house to do the work, very black, very lazy, very willing. They soon found that my demands were few – when I was not at the studio I was sunbathing and going to bed early. I think they were disappointed in me. The film that Paramount had concocted was called *Fatal Lady* – a ghastly title. Walter Pidgeon was in it – I think it was one of his first films, if not his first; it had quite a good story, despite its lurid title, and an outstanding opera sequence. Recently my niece wrote that she had seen it in a little cinema in New York, where they specialise in nostalgia and very old films.

There have been three unresolved friendships; the story of them belongs here, because Oleg Conrad, the third of them, came into my life at that little house in Santa Monica, and I never saw him again, or knew what became of him. He was a rosy-cheeked, sturdy little boy who loved to draw and for some strange reason found his way to me almost every day when I was not at the studio: we would sit beside the pool under the sun umbrella and talk and talk, and I think if I had ever had a son I would have wanted him to be like Oleg. He gave me his photograph when I left: 'To my friend'. I wonder if he is an artist, where he is, if he is happy and successful, or if the Second World War claimed him as it did so many others.

The first of these unfinished encounters was that young Italian on the train to Munich, when I was twelve and travelling with Mother and Father. He kept tuberoses in his handkerchief pocket, and wore chamois gloves, and when we went into tunnels, smelled the tuberoses. I suppose I naturally stared at this dark-eyed, pale phenomenon; months later Father received a long letter in Italian at his office, addressed to me: it was a romantic unbelievable remembrance of that non-meeting on the train. I had not been conscious of it at all – no word had been spoken. I don't know what my father answered. I have the letter to this day, signed Oreste Basilio.

The second encounter was at St Moritz. He was a Russian, his name was Beylin: his mother lived on the Place Vendôme in Paris; he played tennis with an amber rosary half hanging out of the pocket of his white flannels. He was preposterous . . . and asked me to elope with him (I was still only nineteen, after my first opera season and a disastrous marriage) saying he'd have coach and horses at midnight waiting at the Kulm Hotel to take me to Paris to his mother and then to Russia, where he'd build me a theatre. I fortunately didn't believe a word of it, but I *did* look out of the window at midnight, into the starry Alpine night. At the great doorway of the hotel, a large glossy limousine shone in the lamp-light. The maître-d'hotel told us the next day that he had gone . . . and that he was a millionaire, among other things. Heigh-ho. He was older than I was, so I imagine he has departed to an ice-hot Russian heaven. Of the three unfinished symphonies, I like Oleg best.

Tim came over and spent two months with me, and we both grew to dislike Hollywood and all it meant, more and more. The pearly dawns and rafts of interlocked seals singing in their wooing ecstasies as the Pacific tide swept them along, were very far from the publicity-mad studios and stars – it was a divided world; and only Garbo seemed to know the secret and put up her fences.

I finally had to realise that Basil would never come back – it was three years since his elopement to New York with his young actress – so I decided to go to Nevada after the film was over, where I could, by staying three weeks in residence, get a very quiet divorce on the grounds of incompatability. Of course, if we had been married in England, I could not have done this, but as far as England and Basil's Catholic Church were concerned, I was not married to him at all. It was a strange experience living on a ranch, away from so-called civilisation; I rode for hours every day with long treks into the plains and mountains, comfortable in a western saddle. A dude cow-boy and his wife led about six of us on trails, past herds of wild horses, only their heads showing above the long grasses, the sun so strong that if you left a white glass bottle propped against a stone, you could come back in a week and find it had turned to church-window blue or violet.

One evening a car drove up to the ranch-house. It was Stokowski, who took me to dinner at a small restaurant, where an orchestra was playing in a very 'Palm-Courtian' manner, much to his distress. I often wonder what would have happened if they'd known who he was! I wondered why he had come – as he talked endlessly about Axel Munthe's *Story of San Michele* which he had just read; and then the truth came out. I shall never know why I was the privileged listener to his absolutely overwhelming passion for Greta Garbo. What happened about it I don't know. I never saw him again – except from a seat in the concert hall when he conducted – because I left for home and England a week after his visit.

*   *   *

Tim was at Southampton to meet me – and we planned to motor to the South of France for a short holiday. I had been asked to play in *Tovarich* earlier, but could not get back in time, so I accepted a play translated from the Hungarian (again!) by John Balderston, called *Farewell Performance*. A title enough to kill any actress or any play.

Before the play, there was a film to do and a new flat to move into. The film was a version of *Glamorous Night* to be made at Elstree. The English studios had not tackled a musical of that size before, so it was quite an adventure. Otto Kruger came over to play the King and Maire O'Neill played my theatre-dresser – very adorable and full of gin by eleven in the morning. Brian Desmond-Hurst directed: I remember he had an eczema on his hands and had to wear white cotton gloves the whole time. The film ran for twelve weeks at the Regal, Marble Arch – a fine record in those days – and lately had a showing at the National Film Theatre. In New York it goes on T.V. quite often as an 'oldie'.

After the film was finished, Tim and I drove in his Ford V8 to the South of France. I knew Paris well, but had never been to the south. It was fun, through mountains and vineyards stopping at small inns, before the great motorways took over; and there were picnics by the roadside, out-of-the-way villages, days of dust, bathless, eating omelettes under grape-vines in shadowed cobbled courtyards, laughter, feeling free in an uncommitted companionship. Then I saw St Paul, the walled village in the hills behind Nice, and fell in love with it – and swore I'd come back some day. It was one of the four or five walled hill villages from the time of the Cardinal Wars. Stories have it that an attacking army from Vence fled in a panic from St Paul which, having no cannon balls, fired black cherries from the one cannon on the ramparts and spattered the advancing Vencoises with what they thought was their dark life's-blood! There was only a country road winding up to it through olive trees, then – no buses or tourists or fast cars. I was thrilled to see the rustic homes of Braque and Chagall, with Renoir's neglected house and olive grove nearby, and the cypresses standing like black exclamation marks in the rust-coloured landscape.

Tim was a good companion. The men I've known who had loving natures, but could not love women completely, I have found were comforting friends. I suppose that my unhappy experiences with the total male made such relationships a relief, and rewarding.

When I got back to London, in the summer of 1936 rehearsals started. *Farewell Performance* opened at the Lyric in

September, with a party afterwards at my new flat: Ivor, Noel Coward, the painters John and Paul Nash and John Balderston were there. We all felt the play was a flop – it ran for some weeks – but we knew, somehow, that it didn't matter. The only talk those days seemed to be about the war in Spain, and the rumblings of what was happening in Germany, and Oswald Mosley asking young men to put on black shirts and march with him. I had always been a non-political person: too occupied, too self-engrossed; and unlike most of the young of today, I was brought up to believe blindly that those in power could take any crisis in their stride. Overnight, I became piercingly aware of the world around me, the threats, chaos, false gods. Theatre – yes; work – yes, but with a new dimension that made every word, and gesture, sharper; a demand in myself to find the reason and meaning in things that I'd been taking for granted.

Then early in December came the traumatic experience of hearing Edward VIII's abdication speech on the radio. Four of us were in Tim's flat and sat in stunned silence. The familiar pattern of life in Britain was shattered and has never gone back to that accepted unthinking design of the thirties. Through the weeks preceding it, the thought that the Government or the King could possibly demand or take such a drastic decision was inconceivable. It all added to my own personal feeling of insecurity.

I think I have always been searching for a conviction: somehow to be dedicated, to have complete faith. The theatre seemed too egocentric for this; I was sure that the theatre could not be the whole of life, for this would end in emptiness when the footlights went out. I envied the writer, the painter, the musician – who in their self-contained creativeness could make a world of their own.

Love, as I had thought it would be, seemed to be beyond my reach. I had been so wrong, so mistaken – a failure, in fact. I turned to Father Hickey, a gentle old Jesuit priest I had known for some months, who had great patience with me. I studied with him, tried very hard, but Catholicism was not the answer. I wanted warmth and human involvement. I had no faith in myself as a person. I woke up one morning and knew that I had to see and talk to my own father again, to identify with his reasonableness, his sense of values. So I set sail on a May morning in one of the new huge ocean-liners. As I walked the deck I noticed a pale man watching the cliffs disappear. He looked up and his dark eyes shot arrows at me; arrows barbed with an acid and compassionate curiosity. I walked past, knowing I would talk to him before the voyage was over. It sounds like a Victorian novelette, or a very bad movie, but these things have happened to all of us.

The second day out he introduced himself – the Reverend Dick Sheppard. He was ill and tired and travelling with a man who took care of him, as he was subject to dreadful bouts of asthma. His wife had just left him, breaking a long marriage. One of the thousands of Women's Clubs in the United States had offered him a big fee to talk to them. He had never been to New York and needed a change from Amen Court and St Paul's where he was Canon. His fame had become world-wide when he preached for years from St Martin's in Trafalgar Square and he was the first church-man to broadcast, and use the radio as communication; to all the soldiers in the 1914–18 War he gave hope, and humour, and warm understanding. And to everyone who was fortunate enough to have his friendship he brought what they most needed. He proved Christianity by living it.

In those last six months of his life, in which I knew him, he stretched my mind and spirit to waking point. I think of those strange 'flower children' of the sixties, searching, seeking out gurus, and quiet places – he would have understood them, just as he did the thugs and vagrants. This quiet, plump man, dressed in his dark grey clerical suit, rejected no-one; reached the hearts and minds of a generation, and offered great humility, wisdom and laughter; if we only could have learned to accept it. Most of that voyage was spent listening to his arguments that tried to wean me from any Catholicism that still haunted me. His whole moral vision seemed wide, and free, and boundless.

While he was in New York, I saw him almost every day and introduced him to my parents; they were as puzzled by him, as he was curious about them. He wanted to see all aspects of New York life – the sordid little bars on side-streets as well as the most expensive restaurants. I have never had such a hectic week. One day he spent a fortune on a yellow taxi-cab going from one 'speak-easy' to another – he did not drink, so he pretended at each dangerous dive that we were looking for someone. He sat at the bar, sipping soda-water and talking to the very shady characters in the semi-darkness, while I sat perched on a bar-stool, numb with fear of what might happen at any moment: muggings, or police raids, but everything was calm and quiet, strangely so. Then one more spree the next day at a luxurious Park Avenue hotel and he went on his way westward to lecture to his Ladies' Clubs.

After a wonderful week with Mother and Father I went back to England. I never saw my father again.

*   *   *

The summer passed slowly. Tim had found new and old friends and needed me no longer.

This was the early trial television period, where one's face was painted pale ochre, with plum-coloured lips. I stood in a chalked circle to sing a Noel Coward song. People had to go to radio shops to see what happened. Sharing all these horrors were several performers chosen to test out the new miracle. We all looked ghastly, like Frankenstein monsters. Gradually after that, Alexandra Palace became a bee-hive of a new art and after the war I went back again and again, the plays and technicalities getting better and better. It was like being in at the beginning of a new world.

I met Dick Sheppard once or twice a week; we would lunch in a little French restaurant in Dover Street. When he went to France, to visit an old priest there, he would telephone me, to make sure I was all right. Letters came from him . . . daily little notes full of advice and concern. My disbelief that I was important to him prevented me from becoming more depedent on him and I knew of his deep involvement with many people. His American visit had been a great disappointment to him – the Ladies' Clubs had not paid him, and of course he did nothing about this. Ever since he had been a young minister London had been his city, but he loved Canterbury, one of his stopping-off places, where he had been Dean of the Cathedral from 1929 to 1931; and he is buried there. In 1934 he founded the Peace Pledge Union; his passionate wish for peace in the world must surely have been born of his experiences in the First World War, and his dedication to the human condition. I am glad he did not live to see the Second World War and to know that all he believed in so deeply meant nothing in terms of politics and power.

At this time H.M. Harwood asked me to do a play, *The Innocent Party*, to open at the St James's Theatre in the early new year. So on a weekend in October I took the script away with me to the country to read it carefully. On the Monday morning I was handed a newspaper with headlines announcing Dick Sheppard's death during the weekend. When I arrived back at my flat, a letter had been pushed under my door. It was marked 'delivered by hand' and had been written from the Deanery, Amen Court on Saturday evening. A despairing letter, but even so speaking faith in the joy of living. The papers said he had died of an asthma attack, at work at his desk. So little did they know of him.

At St Martin's in Trafalgar Square two days later the dawn broke as a sudden chorus of starlings flew in through the open church door. Only a few people had watched there all night as I had. Rose Macaulay was one of them. As the sun came up, all the night workers in London seemed to come in and file past his coffin – taxi drivers, office workers, coffee stall keepers, prostitutes, Covent Garden porters, cleaners, bus drivers; some tattered vagrants, some all night drunks; the most motley crowd imaginable, walking past his coffin. No words can describe that silence of grief and love, as the early sun shafted down into the heart of his church, touching the lilies so that they outshone the flames of the candles.

Some days afterwards Dick's secretary telephoned me and asked me to come to Amen Court, St Paul's, to choose whatever books I wanted from his library. I crept around the room looking at shelf after shelf and my hand finally closed upon the first proof copy of *The Psalms for Modern Life* with drawings by Arthur Wragg; introductions and corrections in Dick's handwriting, and his book-plate. As I took the book, another hand reached out. A small man with great eyes and an open smile said 'I wanted that too'. From that moment 'Raggy' and I were friends, through long years till his death in 1976. Our friendship became an extension of my relationship with Dick. One felt one could do anything, think anything, say anything, and be understood, even if not approved.

He was a fine artist; although known best for his political cartoons, he illustrated many books – *Cranford, Moll Flanders, Ballad of Reading Gaol* among them; as diverse in style as his understanding. He was as near a saint as I shall ever know. Anti-war, anti-racialism, anti-anything that would curb the human spirit – he would say: 'I'm on everybody's side!'

That autumn I was often at his studio in Baker Street which he shared with his artist friend Fred Roberts-Johnson and an old English bull-dog called Nelson, plus a Jeeves-ish man-servant, Leslie. Raggy would stand at his drawing-board, working all evening, as we talked, laughed and listened to music. Nelson, half in and half out of his basket, his great undershot jaw resting on his paws, growled in discomfort. He had perpetual indigestion, I think, and was a very smelly dog.

When Raggy walked home with me at night across Grosvenor Square to South Audley Street, Nelson would go into every doorway, insisting it was home-ground. I always expected to see the Union Jack painted on his broad chest, he looked so like the proverbial symbol of Britain in the cartoons.

Raggy was making money doing the weekly back page advertisement for *Punch*; I think it was for de Reszke's cigarettes at that time – anyway, he hated it, but had to be kept at it to pay the rent. His sharp cartoons were always accepted by the newspapers, but he could not make a living by them. Much later in life he designed many sleeves for classical records and had great ideas about making short, Disneylike films of stories and poetry for schools – the project never came to anything – but I saw his animation slides from *The Lady of Shalott* to the opera of *La Bohème*, all worked out . . . People were much more important to him than his own well-being and he tore himself to pieces helping lost causes and lost people.

Rehearsals started for *The Innocent Party*. Cecil Parker, Basil Radford, Elizabeth Allen were in it and I played Cecil Parker's Peruvian wife, complete with heavy accent, unused to British ways and means. It was a friendly company and Harwood and his wife Tennyson Jesse, splendid to work for. We toured for a few weeks, and the North of England and Scotland were full of Christmas festivities. We arrived in Edinburgh with only two or three weeks to go before the opening in London at the St James's Theatre.

That cold winter afternoon I went to the theatre, the Lyceum; Maudie was already in the dressing-room. It had been a glorious day – the castle etched like an old engraving against a frosty blue sky. I had walked the Royal Mile and had bought six ruby-red glasses in one of the antique shops; the winter wind had whipped through the grey alleyways up and down the Mile. My eyes felt washed and blinked at the blaze

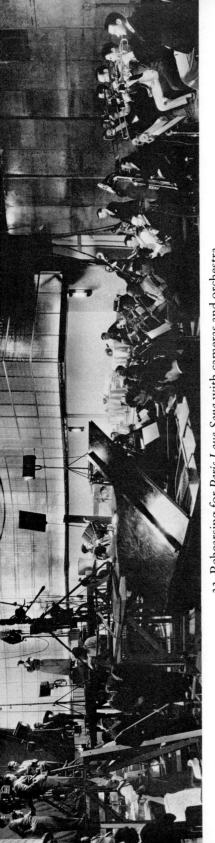

33 Rehearsing for *Paris Love Song* with cameras and orchestra

34 The luggage label drawn for me by the film crew of *Paris Love Song*, on leaving to start rehearsals for *Glamorous Night* in London

35 With Trefor Jones, Olive Gilbert, Barry Jones (in the box on the right), and chorus in the opera sequence of *Glamorous Night* showing Oliver Messel's set for the State Opera, Drury Lane, 1935

of dressing-room unshaded bulbs. Maudie had put a pile of letters beside my make-up and a huge bunch of roses, with a thick letter propped among thorny stems. The sender was no-one I knew. He had evidently seen *Glamorous Night* several times and wrote that he played my records every morning while he shaved. He lived on the Borders and was coming to the theatre that night – and asked if I would receive him after the performance.

I left the theatre to go back to the Old Caledonian Hotel, only a few steps away, for a rest before the play. As I was having tea the telephone rang, announcing a call from New York. My heart missed a beat and when I heard my mother's voice I knew before she told me what I was to hear. My father had died suddenly that day – in his office, at work, alone; even his secretary was out at lunch. Mother's voice sounded strong and she assured me she was all right. There was nothing I could say. I had a job to do – a silly comedy; all I could hope for was somehow to get through that evening without anyone knowing or offering sympathy. I cannot remember getting to the theatre, or the performance. Only that after it, Maudie told me that she had received a cable and had told the cast. Cecil Parker knocked at my door after the play and said how sorry they all were and thanked me for going through with the performance.

Back in a dark hotel room, I battled with the realisation that I wouldn't see my father again or hear his admonitions or praises, or know his steadfastness. One of the certainties of living was cancelled out, forever. My mother would manage very well – she had my sister and grandchildren with her, and many friends. So the distance between us would not matter to her over-much.

The next day was another wintry one; at about eleven o'clock the reception desk rang me to say a gentleman had called. I thought it was someone from the theatre, pulled myself together and went down to the lobby. A tall, lean man was waiting: very blond, unmistakeably a Scot; in full evening dress under a heavy tweed coat – altogether rather rumpled and obviously rather shy. In six months I would be married to him, but that morning I thought he was mad – or, at least, unreasonably eccentric. The explanation was forthcoming. He had, he said, been so excited over the prospect of seeing me in the play, and meeting me, that he had crashed his car, a Sports Jaguar, when he left the theatre. His companion, a schoolteacher from Selkirk, had had to take the last train home – I can imagine her fury – but he had stayed overnight and so had to present himself in his evening clothes, unshaven, and would I forgive him? Of course I did, but told him I was in deep distress, whereupon he turned pale and apologetic and left very quickly. An hour later my room at the hotel was filled with flowers from him.

There followed six months of the most hectic and instructive courtship. Besides continuing my job in the theatre, I learned to ski, climb mountains, fish, share music, painting, photography and Alpine pleasures with Jock – things I had always loved and wanted to do, but had forgotten in a theatre-bound existence. I met his typically Scottish family, living in the loveliest Border countryside (his mother had her doubts about me, but his father liked me;), his brothers and sisters, and later Jock's own children, twin girls, who lived in the south of England with their mother. His marriage had been a very brief one. I think he really loved his non-responsible life; he had been born with several golden, or at least silver, spoons in his mouth; travelling where and when he wanted to, doing as he liked. He once told his sister he would not have married me if I had had to be dependent on him, financially or morally. This freedom between us blossomed into a good, if sometimes hurtful relationship. He was the eldest son and the designer of textiles in his family's woollen mills, working as he wished which was fairly continually, apart from his passionate ski-ing and climbing and photographing in the

Alps. And his flying; under his supervision, and a teacher's of course, I learned to fly too, and only the war stopped me from becoming a pilot of a Moth Minor. If I want to feel nostalgic, I take a look at my white leather flying helmet, slightly rusty around the ear-phones that I keep wrapped in tissue paper, along with other relics.

While I was still playing at the St James's, Jock wrote every day from Scotland, and also from Zermatt, where he went to climb Monte Rosa, near the Matterhorn. His great friend was an Austrian guide, Arnulf, and every year, since Jock had started ski-ing, they had made long snow tours. I realise now that his constant thought of me, and his decision to cut his usual winter adventure short, must have been a very decisive step for him. When he got back to his tweed-designing in Scotland he would motor down in seven hours after work on Fridays. We arranged a holiday in March, in a remote village on the Isle of Skye, thinking no-one would see us or find us there. When we walked into the little inn, we found John van Druten, the playwright, sitting in front of the log fire. He said he retired there whenever he wanted to write a play; but he kept our secret. We climbed through snow-storms, slept on the most uncomfortable damp straw beds, ate haggis and kippers, and decided to get married.

I still had the flat in South Audley Street – and Jock would spend the weekends there. Raggy came, and Tim, and Ivor; I can't think of people more poles apart from each other – but it worked, somehow. Then we found a seventeenth-century cottage near Wadhurst; 'Partridges' it was called, with a stream, a bluebell wood, a large field and a big barn, made into a studio. I rented the largest concert-grand piano I could find to put there – the house itself was too small to hold it. It was low ceilinged and beamed, and poor Jock cracked his skull practically every time he walked through a doorway.

We settled in happily for the two or three days a week he could come down from Scotland and I could be free of the theatre. The play at the St James's had come off after a nice run and my mother came over to see us married. We had some lovely times with her: *Rosenkavalier* at Covent Garden, concerts and plays, and then on July 1st 1938 very early in the morning, we finally smiled at each other in Caxton Hall. We had managed to escape all the reporters, except one who scooped the story which was no news by that time to anyone.

Jock and I went to Norway for a belated honeymoon. He knew Norway very well, spoke the language, and had many friends there; so it was a thrilling visit. I loved the country and its people – the first sight of the fjords, the gliding oily black waters lit by the midnight sun, even the huge mosquitoes; the bilberries, the dried fish for breakfast, the creamy beige country ponies, the featherbeds; the waterfall at Fössli, Peer Gynt's grave (I never knew he was a real person), the double and triple out-house amenities, so that the farmers could talk over their problems together while communing with Nature – the goats following all the way down the mountainside; the sea-bathing on beaches where no-one bothered about swim-suits; and walking across the glaciers – in July still frozen solid, with the skiers coming in for a huge dinner at five o'clock, and a nightcap of tea laced with aquavit. And in Oslo and Bergen the theatres and opera, the parks and palaces.

We had our difficult moments. Jock's mother had brought him up in a staunch Victorian conviction that if a woman enjoyed making love she was not a 'nice' woman. It took quite a lot of persuasion to make him believe otherwise – but when he did, he certainly made up for lost time.

When we got back to England, Scotland, and London, and the cottage, our life took on a pattern; both of us had work to do – and the country weekends were full. Jock's father and sister came, and Raggy, and Christopher Hassall; and of course my mother stayed as long as she wanted to – but she always went off to Switzerland very quickly. She really hated the country; I remember her walking up the lane in a trailing chiffon dress and high-heeled shoes, a look of complete misery on her face, until I brought her back to a comfortable armchair. She also hated any form of domestic pets and particularly cats, which have always shared my household. They, and my Chinese robin, who had to be fed on blue-bottles, and sang like a nightingale, disgusted her.

While I was in Edinburgh that autumn Ivor was there also for several weeks with his company. He telephoned one day, and when we met he had on what I called his secret smile, and whip-lash look. That day *The Dancing Years* was thought out. The story he had in mind was a totally new and unsentimental approach to a musical, about a Jewish Viennese composer, a victim of the Nazi régime, and his mistress, a singer at the Opera House. I could hardly wait for rehearsals, which were to begin in February. Jock was excited and pleased. He was only unhappy whenever I suggested leaving the theatre to be with him – he had fallen in love with me behind the footlights and was determined to keep me there. We often discussed it. I tried to be amused by this, but it worried me a lot.

In January, before rehearsals, we went to ski in Sedrun, in the Engadin, staying at a little hotel, full of Dutch people (they understandably have a special passion for high places). Jock went off daily on ski-climbing expeditions, while I had about seventy bruising falls a day, and enjoyed it enormously. We climbed up one morning to a mountain hut; it took three hours – there were hardly any ski-lifts in 1939 – and we buckled seal-skin strips along the skis to keep us from sliding backwards while climbing. We were a party of about ten, with a guide. It was a gorgeous day in the burning sun; there seemed to be no cares in the world.

Coming down should have taken half an hour, but I swerved into deep snow and went headlong. The next thing I knew I was on a stretcher made of four skis, being carried down the mountain to a waiting sleigh. The guide and Jock (absolutely furious) got me to the hotel where I was told to bathe the ankle in 'Essigsauerertonerde', – whatever that might be – and wait and see. Needless to say next morning the ankle was the size of a balloon and deep purple, so Jock got a car and drove me to a convent hospital in Ilanz, where they found I had a double fracture. The nuns set it and said I must stay there for three weeks. Panic set in; I had to get back for rehearsals, and therefore should not have risked ski-ing anyway. I begged them to put a light plaster on the foot so that I could go on my way. Then I remembered that Juler, Tante Sophie's son – my cousin in Zurich – had told me of a marvellous specialist who did not believe in plaster for breakages, so we rang him and were off to Zurich the next day – poor Jock absolutely fuming that his ski-ing holiday had been spoiled.

We went to my cousin's house on the lake, and he was full of kindness and concern. The specialist came and said the nuns had set the fracture beautifully. I was to do exercises in the bath for ten minutes each day and re-bandage it. He made me promise not to go to 'hospital or Harley Street' for ten days and then to have another X-ray and start walking! All this I did, after arriving at Victoria Station next day in a wheelchair, to the amusement of the porters there who were used to the ski-accident traffic and treated me to some bawdy remarks. My own doctor agreed to the treatment – though he was dubious about the outcome. Jock and I had leased a little house in Belgrave Mews West by that time. It was like a small cottage, and we had a maid called Josephine who took care of us. Jock deposited me, leg in plaster, and left for Scotland to resume his ski-ing holiday, while Josephine helped me into the bath each day and I practised the insistent routine and got through the pain, while I learned the script and the music of *The Dancing Years*.

I told Ivor I had sprained my ankle but would be quite ready for rehearsals, which I was. But I don't know how I stood the pain of the three weeks that preceded them; and the great waltzing finale of the play was agony for me, well into weeks of the performance. We opened on March 23rd 1939.

The cast was splendid. Ivor himself, of course, playing the composer, Rudi Kleber; Anthony Nicholls, Peter Graves again, Roma Beaumont – an enchanting Grete – and Olive Gilbert playing my singing teacher with great comedy sense and that gorgeous contralto voice. Our duet in the first act, 'Wings of Sleep' in Ivor's best Brahmsian idiom, literally stopped the show on the first night – the applause went on into the next act. Leontine Sagan directed again and an added bonus was Freddie Carpenter's choreography.

The Dancing Years was an overwhelming success. The play itself, set in the Vienna that loved and sang in the years before the war, was – as Ivor had first outlined it to me in Edinburgh – the story of Rudi Kleber and Maria Ziegler, the principal singer at the Theater an der Wien, and the misunderstanding which led to their parting. But Ivor added a Prologue depicting the Nazi Headquarters, surrounded by red and black swastika banners, with Rudi Kleber being sent to a concentration camp; and an Epilogue where Maria, married to a Nazi official, manages to free him and they meet again, old, but remembering all that has happened.

It was courageous inasmuch as it used ideas that had not been thought of as material for an operetta. Again there was a sad ending – the scene where Rudi meets his illegitimate son and the sense of what was pending. Perhaps it was that needle of truth in what Ivor foresaw that made the play and its music more exciting. Drury Lane blazed again. The music was of his best; it was a delight to sing – even if it demanded three octaves in the voice. Thank goodness I still have the original recordings. It is sad that audiences did not see the Prologue and Epilogue as originally written when the play re-opened during the war, and went on for so many years. Without that beginning and end, it became a charming Vienese fantasy, but lost its main impact.

I had bought a small mini-Morris car, and every Saturday night Fenner, my gardener at the cottage, would drive it up to the stage door to take me back to 'Partridges' till Monday afternoon. As we approached the cottage, in the dark unlit country lane, the only sound would be the chirping of that Chinese robin in his cage on the window sill, who seemed to know the sound of the car's arrival at midnight, and would burst into song. I knew that summer was a peak of happiness; all of us knew it. I know it now, even more surely.

The cottage was a magical place, the Sundays filled either with friends who came down from London, or bicycling all around the countryside on our own. Rebecca West, who lived nearby, asked us over. Her guests were so clever that I turned into a shy clam – Jock, who had no such inverted vanity, always enjoyed himself enormously. I remember it because I admired her so much, and whenever I meet someone I admire intensely, I collapse into total inadequacy until I know them well. I've really been the ideal hero-worshipper. It was one of those perfect English summers, green as green, with roses all the way; London getting dirtier and dustier, Drury Lane filled to overflowing night after night. There were after-theatre suppers, Royal curtseying, all kinds of audiences and the thousand-and-one responsibilities that belong to a success.

Worrisome rumours; people saying 'It won't happen, it can't happen' – then it happened and at the beginning of September we were at war. That day we had heard air-raid sirens; that night London went dark and every theatre closed. In Drury Lane, Ivor told the small audience to gather close to the stage. We managed to get through the performance, not daring to look at one another. We said goodbye, wondering whether any of us would meet again.

I packed my make-up, took pictures off the wall, looked at my dressing-room for the last time. In the blackout Jock took me to Victoria Station, where we got a train to the cottage, not knowing where or what or how tomorrow would come. We talked all night, and Jock said he would go to Scotland the next day to enlist in the Air Force. I telephoned my mother who was in Paris and she told me she was sailing to the States the next day in the S.S. *Manhattan*. There were radio bulletins all through the night dealing with mobilisation, evacuation, black-outs, air-raid shelters; all of life seemed pencilled through; I thought I would never sleep or eat or think straight again; and yet there was a strange exhilaration. By morning we had packed some suitcases, and made an early start in Jock's car. All the way to Scotland there were bulletins at various garages where we stopped for petrol, or in pubs where we had coffee; and in the afternoon there was an announcement that one of the two liners sailing for the United States that day had been sunk. They did not say whether it was the S.S. *Manhattan* or the *Athenia*: and until the name of the vessel was announced the next morning, I could not care about anything else that was happening. The relief then that my mother was in the ship that was safe, was so great, that I faced up to the problems ahead with a kind of synthetic zest.

4

Interval:
The Lights go out – and on again

From September 1939 to August 1940, was that bleak non-war war. I could not believe in the nightmare that was now Germany. I had known it in my childhood – full of music, laughter, food, the baroque angels of Bavaria and golden sunbursts of its churches, the symbols of a rather bucolic and childishly arrogant people. It seemed as though everyone except the inner ring of politicians had been kept miserably unaware of the Nazi tidal wave approaching.

After a week in Scotland I came back to London; Jock had enlisted, been refused as a pilot, and was commissioned into RAF Intelligence. He had to go on various courses. His first posting was to Northern Ireland. I joined him there for a little and did some concerts; a big one, near Aldegrove, in a hangar, freezing cold; and one back in Edinburgh at the Usher Hall. Then I came back to London and arranged that our country cottage should be given over to London evacuees. After several weeks of severe blitzing (even a piece of burning shrapnel plunging through the skylight onto my bed while I was sheltering in a downstairs bathroom, with the cat) and coming out into the smoke-filled early mornings to find the houses around sometimes opened up like hinged doll's-houses; and watching the slow-moving, clanging fire-engines coming past, the exhausted men clinging on with blackened faces after a whole night on duty in raging city blazes, I finally put all the furniture into storage where it was destroyed by a bomb two nights later; I closed the Mews house, and our faithful Josephine went to work at a munitions factory.

The theatres started re-opening in London, but I had made up my mind to do a war job, no matter what. Somehow, maybe foolishly, I felt it was too easy to do what I loved doing. I wanted to fight my war the hardest way I could find – I saw young people all around me having to leave their husbands, and parents, and friends. To stay in the theatre would have meant an unchanged consciousness, and I felt life was horribly changed. I could not explain it – nor could my theatre companions understand it. Ivor wanted me back with him, ENSA wanted me to tour – but I chose to lose my identity for three-and-a-half years, and become a small cog in Welfare and occupational therapy work at Emergency Hospitals.

My first Welfare job, with blessings from the Ministry of Health, was on the Isle of Islay, Inner Hebrides, where the RAF was newly stationed for Coastal Command and an aerodrome was being built. It was very beautiful; high winds, icy cold, from November until May. A company of officers, four WAAFs, and a lot of airmen, were stationed at Port Ellen which I think only boasted about five hundred inhabitants in a huddled line of little white houses along the shore of a small harbour. There were cliffs where herds of wild goats roamed; seals sunning themselves in hidden coves; and in the early spring wooded groves of daffodils and violets. The incongruity of planes droning on their coastal missions, the occasional high-flying Nazi vultures; the hourly bulletins on the radio; and the constant wondering – when and where the bombs were falling.

That Christmas was snowy and very lonely for the men. One islander, Islay McEachern, became my friend and helped me with the few entertainments which included dances in the

Village Hall, singing to the wheezy legato of a harmonium; he was very musical, very kind, and his mother a great personality on the island. Her many sons were all in the war – all except Islay. I never asked why he was still on the island, but there must have been a good reason. On the WAAFs' free days I would take them with their bicycles across to the Isle of Jura, owned by Lady Astor, who let the RAF fish and shoot there, during their postings on Islay. This was a great help to the feeding problem, as the Ministry of Supply sent us very little, by a small ship that arrived once a week. Chocolate and sausages became the height of gourmet desiring.

Jura was reached by a row-boat ferry. You hoisted a flag on Islay, and if and when the ferryman noticed it, he rowed over from Jura to fetch you. He was a grey-bearded Highlander, a chunk of topaz on a heavy gold watch-chain across his woolly waistcoat. He told me that topaz was found in the cracks of granite rock, just as amber oozes out of trees. The Paps of Jura are three conical hills, like a child's drawing. It is, or was, a Walt Disney island, where deer stood in your path and dared you to disturb them; where plovers rustled only a foot away as you walked past their heathery nests, and hares stood upright, twitching their whiskers, unfrightened. The only danger was during the rutting season – when the stags went wild – if you happened to be in their path, it was best to hide in a ditch till the herd had galloped past.

I learned so much during those months. An elderly woman who owned a house by the sea taught me how to recognise chalcedony, crystal, quartz and cornelian among the pebbles on the beach. She taught me that crystal stays ice-cold no matter how long you hold it, that the way to know chalcedony is to touch it with your tongue and if it is real, your tongue will stick to it – it looks just like a grey black-veined pebble. I got to know many of the airmen and listened to their woes and worries, and flew to Glasgow every few weeks in a blacked-out six-seater plane, to do their shopping. Once we were chased by a German reconnaissance plane, and expected bullets. I met the Head of the Clan on Islay and was shown over the Whisky Distillery that made the famous Islay Mist by Mr Hunter himself. I learned all the Hebridean songs I could, and a few words of Gaelic. After the war, one of my delights was when Islay McEachern came to London for a holiday, and we talked over those days. He wore a bright blue island tweed suit and looked at London in amazement; his eyes still held the light of his wind-swept native paradise.

Apart from official duties, my work included helping with the lambing; learning to drive a car and bicycling miles on Air Force errands. I wondered continually at the beauty of the place; at the small churches built completely round, 'to keep the devil out of the corners'. And then the service days when crates and lifebelts were washed up by the tide, which told us which ships had been sunk out at sea. During these months also, I was involved in a James Bondian episode. I was ordered to organise and sing at a concert one night at a private house high on a cliff above the sea, until a signal came from an officer at the back of the room. While this was happening it seems they had time to search and discover that U-boats were able to re-fuel in the island cove below the house. It was all hushed up and the owners of the house disappeared. I didn't feel I was near enough to the war and what was happening, and was glad when the Hebridean job was done.

So I went back to the mainland, where Jock was waiting for a long-term posting. In Edinburgh I decided to ask for a hospital job. Jock had a few weeks in Fifeshire, then in Wales, and so on, till it seemed he had been posted to every RAF station in Britain. We were together when he got leave every now and then — days spent in tension from Pembroke Dock to Lochinver, where I learned to fish for trout; at that North-West tip of Scotland, the sea is blue as the Aegean, the sands as white and warm; little crofts where old ladies kept bees and the children had never seen trains — only aeroplanes. The sugar loaf mountain called The Beacon, where the sheep slipped and, if caught by the frost, all made a sad woolly heap at its base. Jock asked me to go back to the United States, as I still held an American passport. Maybe this was a protective gesture, but I would not do this, and so finally when he was posted to Iceland, I took the hospital appointment, and my real war started.

An emergency hospital near Peebles, where I was asked to work, consisted of a stripped and disinfected manor house and a score of pre-fabricated wards and offices built in the vast grounds. My hours were from eight in the morning till midnight. I could have slept in, but leased a workman's cottage nearby, where on my day off – one a week – I painted, listened to music and marvelled at a world that seemed lost forever. The Tennent Management sent a telegram asking me to play in *The Little Foxes* in London; I wanted to, but had committed myself to the hospital so had to refuse. I don't think they – Hugh Beaumont and Emlyn Williams who directed – understood the situation. But I was allowed off to do several radio programmes, and had a thirteen-hour journey travelling all the way to Bangor to meet Anna Instone who was producing an hour-long George Gershwin programme, and one called *America Sings*. In between the two, she and I walked in the countryside and almost felt in holiday mood. It was a wonderful break from the war routine of hospitals and blitzes.

The work in the hospital was rewarding. When I had first arrived old Dr Dow called me into his office. When I knocked, and his voice called 'Come away', I didn't know whether to go in or go away. He was very puzzled that I was there to 'Welfare' the hospital. He said that in his day, after a hard day's work, the nurses and staff were glad to go to bed with a book. I persuaded him that times had changed and so was given a nice office, and a free hand, and the title of 'specialist' which entitled me to eat at a table with heads of departments and share the extravagance of mashed potato flavoured with onion juice and very strong tea, which was called supper. Some of those suppers were mad fun, especially near Christmas, when I was directing a revue for the hospital. Laurence Housman had given me permission to use any of his Queen Victoria playlets and we had musical and dramatic talents galore among the staff, from ward-maids to the Head Surgeon. ENSA, at Drury Lane, sent up hampers of costumes whenever I needed them, and Basil Dean, who was then in charge of ENSA, asked if the hospital would be permitted to send its revue to other hospitals. Of course this was impossible, as every nurse and doctor was needed for continual duty. Our great disaster was when a suspected diptheria case prevented a Christmas performance.

Besides dealing with the personal problems that cropped up – from Polish airmen getting the nurses pregnant, to the Matron's stiff neck – I also taught a small ward of children, evacuated from bomb-blitzed Glasgow, as there were no teachers available; and every evening I gave keep fit exercises to the staff. What I had learned as a girl from Alys Bentley, became a god-send to tired nurses. The Matron, Miss McFarlane, a wonderful woman, in full-sail of starch and medals and always longing for Kenya, finally succumbed to the idea of the exercises – I was bidden one day to relieve her stiff shoulder, and felt triumphant. She kept gin in the cupboard of her great office, in the main building, which she doled out to nurses who had their monthly pains. I came in one morning and was given a dose – neat – and felt very odd going about my business. The occupational therapist taught me a lot and I worked with the service-men who were sent to us, disabled, wounded in mind and body. For years after the war I would receive gifts they had made: sheepskin mittens, gloves, carvings, leather book-markers. They break the heart.

I am grateful for the hospital experience and I understand the dedication to nursing. I loved the discipline where devotion to the human condition superseded all personal problems and sentimentality, where to make a violinist, who had had his right arm blown off by a Nazi grenade, feel that it was still possible to face the future, meant success.

When Jock came back to Britain from many months in Iceland, I got leave from the hospital to be with him. He was posted to a hush-hush job in the south, just outside London. We took a house, with a big vegetable garden, and I had an officer and two untidy WAAFs billetted on me. There was no help available, of course, so my days were filled with household chores; gardening, cooking, scheming to find enough food; it was all an odd change-over but it was wonderful to be with Jock again, even though he seemed almost a stranger. I was very much in love with him. His eyes were still the same deep sea-blue. Very occasionally, and almost as if he were eavesdropping on himself, he would speak of love. His words have remained with me like undefined music. He had changed – not towards me – but in his outlook. He seemed totally disillusioned.

I was asked to do many radio programmes, and commuted to London often through early morning air-raids. It was amazing for me, in blitz-wounded London, to see that *The Dancing Years* had re-opened in 1940 at the Adelphi. I felt like Mrs Rip Van Winkle when I passed the theatres; and I felt a vague uneasiness and wondered whether I might not have been of more use staying in my own world. There were some weeks in Bedford, where all the big orchestral programmes of the BBC were broadcast during the war, conducted by Stanford Robinson; I did a lovely music-life of Offenbach, and also a production of his *Grand Duchess*; and so I gradually came back to life. Eric Maschwitz had written a script about Lola Montez – he wanted me to consider it, but I was still deep in war concerns and it was like waking up after a troubled night, to find that music and theatre and all that was still going on, as though nothing had happened. I was living two lives. Late in 1943 I wrote to Ivor, asking him to read the Maschwitz script.

36 and 37 Ivor Novello and myself in our Gypsy Wedding
costumes for *Glamorous Night*

Marie —

id like Dick!
Du bist eine grosse
Künstlerin und
ein prachtvoller
Mensch.

Leo
1935

darling —
my love and
gratitude for
this glamour
and my
prayers for
more flicks!

Ivor
1935

38 The first page of the album of photographs from *Glamorous Night* inscribed for me by Ivor and Leontine Sagan, the director

39 Reading the reviews with Ivor at his country house, Redroofs, after the opening of *Glamorous Night*, 2 May 1935

The letters he wrote back are important, because they cata-
pulted me back to where I belonged. Here they are:

> Darling, you must do Lola Montez – you've been away nearly three
> years and it's too long – what a welcome you'll get and be so glad you
> haven't mixed yourself up with any 'Tattery' in the meantime. One of
> the major tragedies (for me and the theatre) of the war, was the
> breaking of our – let's face it – thrilling association – you were quite
> right about *The Dancing Years* when you said it had a quality which
> makes it independent of the players. It must have, because even
> without you and me they are playing to over £3,000 a week!!! So with
> you and me we'd have had to take Olympia and filled it – *without*
> microphones too! Darling, just as an investment for the future, don't
> get too settled and content to entertain the troops – don't let the magic
> you've got get belittled – it might dissolve into star-dust and that
> mustn't happen. Get back to London and *appear*. I heard Binkie
> [Beaumont] was mad for you to do *Little Foxes* – a magnificent part if
> almost too utter a bitch to be believed – but Lola Montez done really
> well sounds better for you. We have the 1000th performance of *The
> Dancing Years* in eight weeks time after which I'm billing it as 'The
> Advancing Years'!! . . . All my love darling Mary, Ivor.

The next letter, a month or so later:

> Darling – I gave Tom Arnold the script and we had a long talk about it.
> I explained what I intended to do, and while he is mad keen to do a
> show for you, he says that in his opinion this is *not* the one. I said that it
> would mean I should eventually be re-writing the whole thing – to
> which he replied 'If you're going to do that, why not write a complete
> Mary Ellis Show yourself', to which I had no reply! Until today when
> I really think I have got a *superb* idea for you. I can't very well write
> what it is as it would take too long, but I think you'll love it. Tom's
> point is that as you've waited this long for the right thing then an extra
> couple of months is not going to make a vast difference. He talked
> most intelligently about the play – about which I'll tell you in full. Will
> you lunch here at the flat on Thursday and we'll have the afternoon to
> ourselves. While I'm very sorry about the other play – I can't help
> feeling delighted that the idea of your playing at all has been such a
> spur to my sluggish and wanting-in-inspiration war-ridden intelli-
> gence! If I don't hear to the contrary I'll expect you at one o'clock. – till
> then, *All* my love – Ivor.

At about the same time as all this, Jock was posted to London. We had given up the cottage and the Mews house, so found ourselves a flat near Marylebone High Street where the bombs fell with shattering regularity. I did night duties as shelter-warden, and got very little sleep. I had to learn how to deal with child-birth, in case it happened in a shelter; so, besides a thermos of hot Bovril, I went around with nail-scissors (according to the Red Cross the implement most necessary to cut the umbilical cord), a hot-water bottle, and a camp-stove. This, with a tin helmet, made me feel like a war-cartoon, and certainly balanced the glamour of rehearsing Ivor's music for *Arc de Triomphe*. *Arc* was about a young woman, coming from the provinces in France to become a singer in Paris. It took place in the years before the First World War and went on into her very mature years. The early scenes were reminiscent of the opera *Louise* with Montmartre roof-tops and barges on the Seine. The last act was one act of an opera about Joan of Arc set in Rheims Cathedral; I think the best music Ivor ever wrote. Perhaps if he had lived longer, he would have written the full opera. Leontine Sagan was director again; and the costumes were designed by Cecil Beaton. At the dress rehearsal Ivor stormed up to the stage and tore the sleeves out of a dress I was wearing because he didn't like it; I only hope Mr Beaton was told that it was the composer, and not the actress who vandalised that dress! I was thrilled to be photographed by him in four of the costumes for *Vogue*; and found him a fascinating person. His pale, with-drawn personality disguising an electric energy.

Arc de Triomphe opened at the Phoenix Theatre on November 9th 1943. It was a splendid time in the theatre and audiences and actors behaved magnificently. The 'buzz bombs' had started – those awful unpiloted inhuman flying bombs that came chugging, stopped suddenly and, if you were able to count to ten, you were still alive. Sometimes, during the performance, there would be three or four warning sirens. The only thing that happened was that a few more cigarettes were lit in the audience. Finally it got to be an hysterical nightly episode. As I set foot on stage as Joan of Arc the siren would sound; and fear and risibility would make me sing louder and better. No microphones, of course. Peter Graves, Raymond Lovell, Elizabeth Welch — and a host of gallant singers and actors — and Ivor near at hand still playing in another company of *The Dancing Years*.

I cannot remember the exact date in 1943 when C.B. Cochran took over the Albert Hall for his *Seventy Years of Song* in aid of Toc H charities. It was a fantastic event; every artist available, two huge orchestras, choruses, an audience overflowing, Royalty, Army, Air Force, Navy, and fortunately a lull in the bombings. I listened enchanted to the music of Victorian and Edwardian days; and when finally I started the Indian Love Call from *Rose Marie* off-stage and emerged, I was greeted with a warmth and love I can never forget; the years rolled back, just as they did for so many of us that night. In the third part of the programme, I had to sing 'Glamorous Night'; and to sing into that huge hall was like taking ecstatic flight. All the 1914 war songs, and then the 1939 ones — ending after three hours or more with over a thousand voices singing 'Jerusalem'. It was one of Cochran's great shows and for one blacked out night at least, lifted everyone into blissful limbo.

At Christmas that year Jock was called to Scotland, so I went to Redroofs, Ivor's country house. Boxing Day of course meant two performances and we whizzed up to London in the Novello car — that ration-fuelled car which was going to be such a sad and destructive reason for regret in the months ahead.

A strange thing happens to the spirit, living with a sense of prophetic loss. No day or night passed that one did not *expect* a street, a building, indeed a whole town, to be demolished. And no goodnight or 'see you tomorrow' that did not bear the stamp of possible finality. Against this there was the cosiness of enforced close quarters in shelters and queues and the intimacy of the shared fearful optimism of civilians at war. Looking back, I don't know how we did it.

Some of the things that happened at that time seem like nightmares, now. One night, a great fire started from the bombing of the US Headquarters in Bryanston Square. Jock and I spent four hours on the roof of our building, shovelling hot shrapnel away from the chimneys and sky-light. When I got to the Phoenix Theatre one evening, there was only an open space of rubble beside it where a big building had been the day before. This released lots of rats and mice into the cellar of the theatre, so we had to start keeping cats there at night. The cellar had been made into a changing-room as the theatre did not have enough dressing-rooms, and some of the boys had to make up there, so the cats spent their nights as guardians in case the rats nibbled at the costumes or grease-paint. I had a cat at the flat too, a striped no-pedigree comic who purred through all the bombings, but collapsed into fur-raised stiff aggression the minute he heard bag-pipes. There was a wartime Scot who roamed the streets playing the pipes – we all got to know his hours of wailing – and my cat's tail was twice its original size most of the time.

Then a tragic thing happened. Ivor was sent to prison for a 'fuel-offence' under the wartime regulations. What happened to him was unjust and unbelievable and he never got over it. He had always been kind and good and generous, and would never knowingly have done anything so unreasonable or so damaging to himself, or anyone else; least of all to his country. He loved Britain uncompromisingly. After his ordeal the public demonstrated their faith in him conclusively when he came back to his *Dancing Years* and received an ovation night after night.

In the meantime, another small death – the closing of *Arc de Triomphe*. So many adventures during it: the French soldier on leave who sent back his Cross of Lorraine to me; the old lady from Normandy who came back-stage and gave me a family heirloom – an exquisite cameo – all because of that rousing song 'France Will Rise Again' in the last scene; these are the things that sustain actors, beyond the significance or triviality of the theatre.

A realistic and delightful note: on the last night everyone knocked at my dressing-room door to say goodbye – there was more than the usual feeling of a closing, as the immediate future was so uncertain for everyone. One very young chorus-boy came in to pay his respects. In an uninhibited Cockney accent, slightly sibilant, he said:

'Miss Ellis, it's about time we closed.'

'O dear – why?'

'Well you know those cats in the cellar? One has pissed in my wig.'

It was 1944. I went straight up to Scotland to be with Jock until some war duty called him elsewhere, and all was well. I loved his family, and I could talk for hours to his father about Edwardian life and listen to his Scottish stories. Their big house was full of character; complete with their old Nanny who for some mysterious reason was called 'Whale', despite her very fragile look and gentle ways.

The war was salting life through with partings and re-unions, but when I was able to be with my husband nothing else mattered. I had long understood that his job in RAF Intelligence would necessarily put up a kind of blind barrier between us. I could never, of course, know where he was going, or why, or what he was doing.

Then some work presented itself. I had always wanted to work for the Old Vic. During the war they were evacuated to Liverpool and playing at the famous Playhouse there. William Armstrong and Maud Carpenter, wonderful Edwardian-minded progressive personalities, were the management of the theatre and Tyrone Guthrie and young Peter Glenville were directing the 1944–45 season. They asked me to open in

August as Ella Rentheim in Ibsen's *John Gabriel Björkman* with two or three other plays to follow. I was over the moon with excitement. To belong to a company again would be bliss. I had begun that way at the Metropolitan Opera House. And to this day, whether it be in opera, or theatre, or films, or television, I feel that teamwork is the blood and bone and the greatest joy in performing; the rest is egocentric and rewarding in another way – and rather old-fashioned now, like those gorgeous solo performances when audiences went to see a Bernhardt, or a Duse, or a Pavlova. That particular special personal adulation seems now to be given to the cacophonic, strident, violent world of the pop-star or footballer; nothing to do with thought; all to do with feverish and sex-frayed nerve-ends. I suppose it's quite splendid in its way.

Rehearsals were in London. Despite the V-2 and V-1 bombs every few hours, the days were seething with activity. The spirit of make-do, and survival, and national exuberance and sacrifice made the atmosphere of the scarred city almost more seductive. My first morning of rehearsal was ushered in by the huge bomb blast at Smithfield Market.

It was an odd set-up. Nancy Price, very many years my senior, was playing, according to Ibsen, my twin sister. To adjust to this, the director allowed himself the licence of making me her younger sister in the great play: which I think took away much of the meaning and tension. Frederick Valk played John Gabriel Björkman and his European accent didn't help. However, nothing could take away the thrill of working in that play. I only wish I could have played it again later. Peter Glenville, who was directing, held me properly in check and the smaller theatre was a restful exercise. Oddly enough no bridge had to be crossed between a 'musical' and a straight play, for the simple reason that I had approached the musicals with the same technique. Being able to take a part, even a minor part, in a musical play is simply a question of having a sense of rhythm in one's self and this same rhythm is a vitally important part of any sort of acting. The questions of 'timing' and of 'pace' and of variations of pace, which are absolutely essential from a 'straight' actor's point of view are all bound up with this question of general rhythm. They are the most important weapons in the armoury either of a tragic actor or an actor of comedy, and I firmly believe that the best practical help to an actor is the study of music.

We were finally ready to go up to Liverpool, and I welcomed the idea of a night without wailing sirens, so when on our arrival we had one of the worst night-raids, I suspected the Luftwaffe of disliking actors. The Adelphi Hotel in wartime was amazingly comfortable – ablaze with lights behind its blackout – and there was even music. A small orchestra of very elderly gentlemen in the lounge played the Warsaw Concerto every evening with more emotional verve than accuracy. The management gave me what was called a 'bachelor suite' – a sort of bed-sitter with a bed hidden in an alcove; I suspect so that I could have guests or rehearsals without fear of offending the morality code. Nothing could have been more of a contrast to my three year hospital sojourn, and I felt almost guilty. Jock was only a short train journey away and I expected to be able to see him often. As it turned out, he was only once able to visit me – on New Year's Eve, 1945. He said I must trust him and that some day I would be told everything. I felt that 'everything' to be mysterious and damaging. But there was nothing I could do; and I realised how much luckier I was than the wives whose husbands were being shot down and imprisoned. But there are many kinds of casualties.

The rooms next to mine were occupied by Malcolm Sargent who was conducting orchestral concerts every week in the new concert hall. Later, I was allowed in to the rehearsals whenever I had time off. One wonderful weekend, Tanya Moiseiwitsch, who was designing the costumes and scenery at the Playhouse, took me to meet her famous father,

when he was playing with the orchestra. It was marvellous.
All the feeling of studentship came flooding back; the years
folded like the pleats of an accordion and I felt again like the
child in the starched party-dress, almost sick with excitement
when Josef Hoffman played Schubert and Chopin for a game
of Musical Chairs at a children's party in 1908. How little does
the typical feeling of hero-worship change.

We started rehearsing *The School for Scandal* in time for
Christmas and the routine of work kept me very busy. I loved
playing Lady Teazle. Henry Edwards played Sir Peter; he and
his wife Chrissie White had been the first popular English film
stars, and still had an aura of nostalgic glamour. I had never
seen them on the screen, but somehow they made me feel I was
in the presence of gentle royalty. There were many strange
meetings because of the theatre, or the war – Liverpool was
very much alive and we all frequented a marvellous café at
lunch time where oysters were cheap.

I knew Jock was much involved in some secret war of his
own, besides the real one . . . but I missed him more even than
when he had been posted far away – and at one mad moment
sent him a telegram, saying I wanted to leave the Old Vic
season and be with him. This was idiotic, as he knew, and I
had a reply to that effect.

After the New Year, the theatre decided to put on Noel
Coward's *Point Valaine*. This play had been done in New
York by the Lunts; even their presence in it failed to make it a
success, but it had the bones and shape of splendid theatre –
quite different from anything 'The Master' had written before; a pastiche, almost a send-up of Somerset Maugham's
South Sea syndrome. It was great fun and a success for the
Old Vic season. Noel Coward and Hugh Beaumont came to
Liverpool for the opening night and I knew they were considering the possibility of a London production. In the *Tatler*
(or was it the *Sketch?*) there were photographs and a eulogy
from Mr Coward himself; I was thrilled about it.

40 With Oleg in Santa Monica, 1936

41 With some of the children evacuated from the Glasgow bombing at the hospital near Peebles, 1942

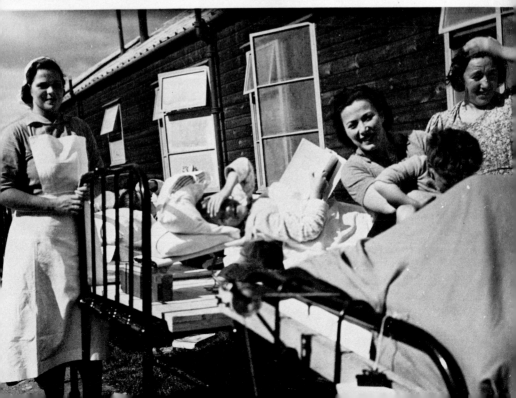

42 With my husband Jock, Switzerland, 1939

43 My broken ankle, the result of ski-ing before rehearsals for *The Dancing Years* – Jock was 'absolutely furious'

44 Act One, 1911

45 Act Two, 1927

46 The Epilogue, 1938

As Maria Ziegler with Ivor as Rudi Kleber in
The Dancing Years, Drury Lane, 1939

47 Mary Morris

48 Romney Brent

49 Dick Sheppard

50 Alan Wheatley

The morning after the opening, I was having early breakfast in my room when there was a knock at the door. A pale, nervous young woman came in. I recognised her as the actress Basil had gone away with, eleven years before. I tried to relax to this odd meeting, and asked her if she had had breakfast; and wondered if she had been to the performance the night before – or if Basil was in trouble, or what. Above all, I admired her nerve, for whatever reason she had come. Over coffee, the story unfolded. A sad moral allegory indeed. She had come to find out if I knew where Basil was! I pointed out as gently as I could that I thought it rather strange that she should be appealing to me, who had suffered through *her* exactly as she was suffering now through someone else. No, I knew nothing about Basil; she left unhappy, and I have always felt tenderly towards her, since that early morning confrontation. How absurd the world of self-deluding females, including myself.

*   *   *

The weeks flew towards Spring. There was an unnerving uplift in the air, because there was a possibility of peace. I had the choice of staying on to play the Queen in *Hamlet*, or leaving for *The Gay Pavilion* by Lipscomb, a play about Maria Fitzherbert, George IV and Sheridan which I decided to accept. It was to be tried out after a short tour, opening in London early in May 1945. The producer was Peter Daubeny. He had a deep passion for the theatre, and was a lovable erudite man; much later his great gift to the public was the 'World Theatre' season every year, which brought to London plays and players from all over the world. He had had a hard war, and had lost an arm, but I never felt that any bitterness invaded his loving kindness.

VE-day was near. The whole company had been able to find rooms in the Norfolk Hotel, Brighton, where we were playing before the London opening. It was packed with all kinds of humanity, mostly elderly people escaping from the bombs in London. The sudden invasion of a group of actors must have startled them, but all that was lost in the carnival excitement of what was happening. For some reason we found Googie Withers and her mother were staying there too. Everyone seemed to be waiting for a great event and Jock telephoned to say he was coming the next day: so I went to the Theatre Royal in a dream, to rehearse *The Gay Pavilion*, the play about George IV set in another Brighton two centuries ago.

VE-night was on May 8th; our hotel overflowed with champagne, and flags, and tears. Jock had arrived from Scotland to be with me and the time stood still. The war was *over*. Not quite – VJ-day was still to come, three months later, in August; a mid-summer evening with everyone going mad in dense crowds in front of Buckingham Palace, or moving like a wave up and down the Mall, singing. Bands playing, flags flying; all who could find an inch of space on the patches of greensward in front of the Palace, waiting for the Royal Family to come out on the balcony time and time again. I marvelled again at the resilience of the human heart and the brave face of bomb-scarred London, glowing in the summer sunset. It was over. It was over. It was over.

Somewhere in one's memory there is a pitchfork that prods and pierces until a fact long hidden is brought to light from under a heap of time. Towards the end of my season in Liverpool, I had had a strange telephone message. I was invited to lunch with a woman I did not know; she said my husband had asked her to talk to me; it was an odd meeting. She explained that I must realise that all personal relationships counted for nothing in view of what Jock was involved in, and committed to . . . At first, I thought it had to do with his job in the war – until she told me bluntly that it was a political issue and that I must understand his reluctance to discuss it, no matter what sacrifices had to be made. She left me sick and bewildered, and determined to find out what had eaten into the heart and mind of my husband. I knew of his swing towards socialism; it was an almost inevitable thing to happen to the eldest son of a fairly affluent and almost feudal family – the old story of the princeling finding out how the other half lives. The war had proved a brutal teacher. I was ready to listen to everything and understand what I could of it; so that when he joined me in the Victory weeks I was glad to find him happy and loving, and I did not want to know anything except the joy of reunion. I had never had the habit of questioning him; in all the years I had never known his reasons for absence or return. So I was determined to wait until he told me whatever I was to know.

We had managed to find a little flat in Dorset Square. I knew that Jock was having trouble in Selkirk, but could not guess of his subsequently leaving the Mill – which, I think, broke his father's heart. One evening he told me he was going to a meeting of some sort. A pale man, with piercing sunken eyes and bad teeth, called for him. My usually immaculate husband took off his tie, put on an old coat and a flat cap and left with this stranger. I didn't know whether to laugh or cry, but from that moment on, I doubted the validity of his committment. If he had to act and dress the part of a communist, the whole issue floundered. So it was a relief in a way; but I knew nothing could be done about it. I should have to see it through.

Friends who had somehow vanished in the war, returned from all kinds of services and places and our home was full of talk and people, with me cooking the best I could with the sparse rationing: and, of course, also waiting for some play to come along, wondering if I'd ever work again; the usual actor's unemployed agony. It was a barren feeling, too; it made me understand war-time heroes who come to no good: if only the spirited best in humanity could carry on into *un*-events; the absence of high tension in those suddenly peaceful days called for adjustments. And all the time I was trying to understand my husband's reasoning – the who, why and where of it.

In January I had a cable from New York to say my mother was ill. Within a few days I knew I had to get to her as soon as I could, so I went to the US Embassy to get a permit – and found I should not be able to return to England soon if I used my US passport which I had kept all through the years, despite the fact that I was now a British subject. Nothing could keep me from getting to my mother, so I gave up the US passport, swearing off, as it were, in front of a lady vice-consul who seemed to think I was a traitor for using only my British passport, even though she knew the distressful reason for my action. Then I sat on the steps of the Embassy, waiting to hear when any plane was going. In a couple of hours I was told I could go that evening on a Clipper, so I rushed back to the flat; no time even to think – Jock could not come with me, but said he would follow.

Somehow I got away. Down by bus to Poole, into the old plane, over Shannon, four engines thumping. Three hours out over the Atlantic I noticed fuel being jettisoned and flames coming out from under one of the wings: and then the over-calm voice of the captain saying we were turning back to land at Shannon. It was pelting with rain and we were taken by bus to a fabulous hotel for the night, while the plane was being mended. The meal that evening, in what seemed a castle, was candle-lit, sumptuous, out of this world to the war-starved passengers: beef, sweets, whisky, wine – unbelievable. And plump waiters saying 'You haven't tasted anything like this in years, have you?' – infuriating, with their juicy Irish voices, leering grins and no compassion; we women passengers were put into a large room in the basement for the night; and next morning were joined at breakfast by the crumpled and unshaven men passengers. Bacon and eggs – we were used to one rationed egg a week – and then off again to get onto the mended plane. The bumpy, uncertain flight seemed to take hours and hours. Finally we landed in New York at about three in the morning. My poor brother-in-law had been waiting since afternoon to meet me – and I was hurried off to my mother's flat.

I was with her for the ten days before she died. She could not speak or move, but the tears often crept down her cheeks as I talked to her and held her hand; we were closer in those last helpless days of hers than ever before. When it was over, Jock came – in the meantime I had been glad to see my sister and nephew and niece again, and the friends who found their way to Mother's flat. I had pangs of tenderness looking through photographs and letters and her personal things – all kept very neatly, and sachet-scented. Her doctor, who had been her friend, seemed very distressed; I knew, even in her late seventies, she had been romantically attached to him. She seemed so vulnerable, somehow, and when I helped the nurse to bath her every day, her body was like a young girl's. And she was so puzzled, and angry to find herself paralysed and unable to speak.

In the afternoons I'd walk down Madison Avenue in the bright winter sunshine and keep looking for bomb-sites and devastations; I'd realise with a shock each time that this was New York, shop windows crammed with food and fashions and things I had forgotten about; my eyes and stomach rejected the fulsomeness, and I felt like a stranger in the city that had borne me, where I had dreamed and studied, and had my career until 1930.

I shall never forget Jock's arrival in New York – dressed in his Shackleton weather-proof clothes, ski-boots, rucksack, with skis on his shoulder; he must have been an astonishing sight for my sister Lucile and her New England husband Arthur Emptage. Added to which, he had been detained for questioning for three hours at the airport, which did not puzzle me as much as it did them. However, when he got dressed up in his super tweeds no-one could say he was anything but the handsomest of tall, blonde Scotsmen, and he could charm even the American birds off the trees. My nephew and his wife were especially interested and we had some delightful times together. Jock needed his holiday, and we arranged to go to Canada for ski-ing. We flew to Montreal from New York, and spent two days there; then to the Laurentians and on by train across Canada to Banff.

We stopped long enough at Calgary to see a beautiful station and a big hotel – the town itself seemed like a bad cowboy film set, but it was only a curtain-raiser at the foot of the Rockies. Nothing prepared me for the monstrous beauty, the overpowering shapes and blinding blue and white of lakes and sky and snow, that flashed into sight, as the train flew westwards. I felt like a Lilliputian.

We went by snow-plough 1,500 feet above Banff to a log cabin ski-house. Sunshine Lodge housed less than twenty skiers. There were two ex-patriate Austrian ski-teachers, and the service was made up of two or three college students who got their winter holiday free for good home-cooking. It was isolated – only mountains in sight, one shaped like a junior Matterhorn. As far as the eye could see not a human track until one made it oneself, having got up to a high field by a tow-rope. Then there were expanses of snow with nothing but the footmarks of hares and bears and foxes and deer to mark the way. Looking back, I'm sure I have a slight Canadian Rocky Mountain complex due to *Rose Marie*.

The Lodge had one living-room with a huge fire-place and the upstairs was divided into cubicles for two, with walls so thin that the sounds of love, snoring, passing wind or whispering had no mystery. Hushed laughter was the most disturbing, arousing all one's curiosity and mild fury. There were two showers, for male and female, a small stove in every cubicle, and a scramble for the breakfasts of griddle cakes, Canadian maple syrup, and strong coffee. Then into the sun, the crystal air spiced with pine, and the snow, snow, snow. I really got too much of it. We made friends with the Konantz's from Winnipeg. She had been the Canadian Head of the Woman's Voluntary Services in the war and had been to England often. Her husband played the guitar and we all sang songs around the log-fire after supper.

Easter was early that year – in March – and as the days grew longer Jock and I knew we had to get home, back to work, and all the post-war problems. Jock lived just above the drowning-line of his ideologies – he was now opposed to everything that he and I had been brought up to believe in. I listened to his new sense of values, his radical change of purpose; but avoided making comment or argument, as I was so afraid it would break us apart. He demanded such complete acceptance of himself, sans criticism or doubt. It was a kind of ferocious integrity that was the pulse of his character; but I was convinced everything would work out.

Back in Britain, while Jock was commuting to Scotland, planning unbeknown to me to leave his father's Mill and start a new kind of life, I was asked to do a season of plays for Anthony Hawtrey at the Embassy Theatre, the season of 1946–47. Before that, in July, Jock decided to take the Jaguar sports car (with me in it) to Switzerland – the seats were so low that I could only have a side-view, like a crab.

We crossed the Channel and drove through France. It was like coming home to all the familiar landmarks – tracing the results of the war all the way. I had literally pinpointed a place on the map because I liked the mad sneezing sound of it: F'Tan. Situated on a high ridge, after Zuoz and Garda, it looked over the Suvretta range one way, and down to Austria the other and was an enchanted place.

On the way, we stayed the night at Rheims and, as a siren woke me in the early morning, I scrambled out of bed, convinced the war was still on, but it was only the French being thrifty and using the siren to tell the townsfolk that the fish market was open. Breakfast was coffee of ground acorns, some very black bread and jam made of plum-stones. The French looked grim and pale, so that, coming into Switzerland all so complacently neutral, one was slightly antagonised. But those unmelting snow peaks proved that no bombs or Nazis could touch or change their constancy. Surely the passion for mountains must be based on our longing for security; even the seas and the deserts change rhythm and shape every hour; the high Alps remain static, tempting us to believe in eternity.

F'Tan was a mass of wild flowers. I would follow Jock on his climbs and into wind-blown crevasses at 9,000 feet and, scared to death, hold a yard of black velvet behind a fire-lily or a rare saxifrage while he photographed them: we brought back slides of every alpine flower, I think. We spent one night in a hut, above 10,000 feet, in order to photograph a bronze gentian at sunrise. I never liked climbing very much, but of such stuff is love made.

*   *   *

The Embassy season started that November 1946, with *Mrs Dane's Defence* by Henry Arthur Jones. It is supposed to be the best constructed play in the English language. Its Victorian-Edwardian moralities and rather seedy plot are amusing and interesting, and that year it had a splendid trial-in-the-study scene, with Henry Oscar wearing down poor Mrs Dane's (my) defence. After that, in February, there was *Hattie Stowe*, a splendid play about Harriet Beecher Stowe by Ian Hay. It was a big production: Milton Rosmer, Anthony Nicholls, Kynaston Reeves and a score more fine actors both black and white − ending up with a scene at the White House, with Abraham Lincoln making that famous remark to Hattie: 'So you're the little woman who made the big war?' That play is among those which I have really enjoyed.

The rehearsals took place in the days that preceded that big blizzard of 1947. We had candles stuck in bottles to rehearse

51 In the opera 'Jeanne d'Arc', Arc de Triomphe, Phoenix Theatre, London, 1943

52 With Ian Dallas in the Old Vic production of Noël Coward's *Point Valaine*, 1944

53 With Peter Glenville, the director, in my dressing room after the first night of Terence Rattigan's *Playbill*, Phoenix Theatre, London, September 1948

by, when there was a power cut. The freeze and snow persisted, and all I could do to help was to offer hot baths at my flat. We all had fun in that hard-bitten winter; discomfort sometimes enhances life, accents the good, just as the war did. One evening, I saw an odd, small person standing at the bar, talking to a large Scandinavian lady. The small one wore what looked like her grandfather's army overcoat, and over-size army boots; and she was smoking a cigar. I said to Tony Hawtrey 'Who *is* that?' and he said 'One of the most talented young actresses in the business, Mary Morris'. I looked again, and saw an expressive face and peacock-blue eyes looking at me with deep hostility.

I had had in those weeks what I call one of my great 'misses'. A letter came, asking me if I would play Gertrude in Laurence Olivier's film of *Hamlet*. I asked Tony Hawtrey if I could be released, but he pointed out that I had a contract with him for the season; so that was that, to my great regret. Eileen Herlie, who had been at the Old Vic with me in Liverpool, was the lucky one who played it. I was miserable about it; it was an invitation to the kind of theatre I longed for. It would, I feel, have re-directed my professional life – but one never knows.

Hattie Stowe had a successful run, and a long tour afterwards. When we were playing in Croydon there was a snowstorm one evening. I somehow managed to get there and was confronted by the stage manager in three different beards, playing all the male parts; we were hysterical and the audience cheered like mad. The blizzard had held up the poor actors in trains, buses and cars. A few weeks later, at one matinée in Bristol, Wilfrid Hyde-White who was playing Gladstone in the London scenes, didn't arrive. He wandered in afterwards saying calmly that he had gone to the races – I felt as though I were in a Marx Brothers film. We heard that Jack Hylton wanted to bring us to His Majesty's – he wanted to make some changes, and to put in some Stephen Foster music, but it did not work out and a lovely play closed at the end of the tour.

While waiting for the third play, a revival of Noel Coward's *Point Valaine* which I had done three years before with the Old Vic, there was a score of television plays; all done live, which in those days was so much more demanding for the actor than the taped plays of today. I know they can be much more technically perfect now, and that actors never seem to be worried or tense, but the excitement of the first night tensions before the camera, the quick changes, the having to do it perfectly, the nerves that somehow give just that added lustre to a performance – that's finished and done with. Now, if there is a mistake, or anything goes wrong, it can be done over again. Among the many television plays I did and enjoyed during those ten years were Shaw's *Great Catherine, The Distaff Side* by John van Druten, *The Indifferent Shepherd* by Ustinov with Michael Hordern and a beautiful play about Turgenev and his love, Mme Viardot, called *The End of Summer*, produced by Michael Barry; then Beverley Nichols' famous play *Evensong*. In preparation for that I had a most lovely day visiting Mr Nichols in the country – his garden, his cats – and the most perfect *crème brûlée* I've ever tasted! He was a charming host, and I had a great thrill televising his moving play about Nellie Melba. The only other primadonna I acted on television was the one in Somerset Maugham's story *The Voice of the Turtle*. How I wish those television plays had been taped then. Much later, I loved being in an Emlyn Williams play, *Trespass*, done at the Welsh Studios and *The Road to Hilda Brown* produced by Peter Willes.

I always want to be on television again; but time is not on my side any more. The medium can be a destructive and dangerous one; perhaps we get to know too much about politics and crime, football and hospitals, but at its best, the fact that one can sit undisturbed and choose what one wants to hear and see, is fine. However, I still believe that having to make an effort to go to the theatre or a concert or an opera, is much more important – that old complex again, that if it's made too easy, it isn't worth having.

Jock had broken with his father, and I was worried and distressed. He came to London and took a job teaching photography for £6 a week at the Camberwell School of Art. Mother had left us a token legacy of £5,000, so we bought the lease of a lovely late-Georgian house in Pelham Crescent – still one of the unspoilt historic sites in London; and, amazingly, I found that my friend Dick Sheppard had known the previous owner of the house and had visited there regularly; an odd coincidence. It seems unbelievable now, but that £5,000 paid for the lease of the house until 1985; it was a beautiful house; I felt happy in it, and when I had to sell it in 1967 I got very little more than we paid for it. The Crescent was alive with theatre people: Emlyn Williams, Margot Fonteyn, Oliver Messel, Cecil Beaton, Eric Ambler and, later, Anthony Quayle. I think if somebody had shouted 'beginners please' the little gardens would have been filled with actors. Emlyn sent me a letter of welcome, and it was all very cosy. Jock fixed up the basement with every photographic gadget and gave private lessons in his spare time. I found myself answering the door-bell to scruffy students and saying 'Downstairs, please'.

Arthur Wragg – Raggy – had come back from teaching all through the war; many of his pupils have since become successful designers and illustrators. Romney Brent had been with the Canadian forces and had come back too, with his beautiful wife Gina Malo and his little daughter to do films in Paris. Many other friends; some new ones of Jock's and old ones of mine. Without Mother and Father I had no ties in America any more; my sister had never been much interested, and the nephews and nieces were too young and busy with their own lives to care at that time. Aunt Emma still lived in Zurich, deep in her eighties, and she and Paul Elsas, a first cousin – and a very modern painter who lived in Paris – were my only remaining European relatives. Since Jock hated France and would never go there, except to whizz through it as fast as possible on his way to Switzerland, I had not seen Paul since we were very young. In his teens he had been

138 Interval: The Lights go out – and on again

faun-like, with curly blond hair. He had married a typical
hard-working Parisienne; they had both been in the Resistance in the war and, having survived, went later to live in
Vence. I made up my mind to find him if I ever reached France
again.

I was holding on to my marriage with everything in me, but
any happiness was overshadowed by that heavy responsibility
that Jock had made of his new commitments and beliefs. He
was right not to include me, as there would have been a
show-down; as it was, the breaking point came so slowly that
I was convinced that some day he'd be as he had been.

It was great fun arranging the house, finding room for the
hundreds of books, the piano, the music, records and paintings I loved, which had been saved during the war. All the
pre-war furniture had been bombed, so we made do with
second-hand finds from the markets. Fun too, planting two
camelia bushes in the tiny back garden, training the old
wisteria, all gnarled branches and purple splendour, to climb
the wall; it was a lovely Spring.

In summer there were scaffoldings all along the front of the
houses. They were being re-painted for the first time since the
war. I was alone in the house – as I often seemed to be, now. It
was a hot evening, and I was ready for bed. I leaned out of the
window, like a mature Juliet, to get some air. Two shadowy
figures walked and stopped on the pavement opposite, and
then a call: 'Mary. It's me, Peter Glenville. I have a script for
you. Read it as quickly as you can. I'll put it through your
letter-box.'

Where had I hung out of a window like that before and
heard something that made my heart gallop? Down the beam
of the years came a sound of harp and fiddle strings, and
once again I saw a pale face looking up at me – only this time it
was an affluent young director offering me one of the best
plays ever written, not a begging musician holding out his hat
for a nickel wrapped in newspaper. My heart bounded. Perhaps I should always lean out of windows?

The moment I read it, I knew it was right. This was it. Now, thirty-odd years on, *The Browning Version* is still considered Terence Rattigan's best play: it was the first of two hour-long plays making up *Playbill*. The second one was in spirited contrast, almost a cartoon-comedy, *Harlequinade*. With any title, that script would have been the gift of all time.

It was good to work with Peter Glenville again; and he and Rattigan made an absolutely gala event of the whole thing. *The Browning Version* dealt with Crocker-Harris, a disillusioned schoolmaster, and Millie, his bitter, unhappy wife. But Eric Portman and I played it as two people so deep in love-hate that they could not leave each other. His scene with the boy who brings him the book he has wanted (the Browning version of *The Agamemnon*), his breakdown, his resignation and Millie's deep deriding worry about him, made you feel those two characters were the epitome of a kind of furious, abiding love. Eric was marvellous as the tragic Crocker-Harris (he never forgave me for being the first one to be asked to do the plays, and reminded me of it every chance he got, I hope with a semi-twinkle in his eye). Marie Löhr played the nurse in the Romeo and Juliet setting of *Harlequinade* and in the try-out weeks, and on the post-London tour, supplied an awe-inspiring Edwardian touch, travelling complete with tea-basket and Pekinese and a thermos of Bovril laced with brandy. Oh, it was gorgeous! Even the hours after the play at night in a hotel suite, thrashing out changes and benefitting by the criticism and direction, and tireless working towards perfection that seemed to galvanise Peter Glenville, Rattigan and all of us, into continual work.

Well, it all paid off. The London opening was more than we had dared to hope for – audiences and critics agreed for once. There is nothing so gratifying as being good in a good play. To be good in a bad one is frustrating, to be bad in a good one, devastating – and an actor always knows, even if he pretends he does not. The rewards and punishments are immense. But this was all good.

Eric and I found a splendid rapport in the play – so that when Rattigan asked me to go to New York with it after the run in London, and they did not ask Eric to go also, I foolishly said 'No'. Only because I was convinced that the particular magic of the play was to keep it intact; even though all of us had had some hard times with Eric, keeping him, literally, on the rails. At Easter he invited me to his enchanting cottage in Cornwall. There I made the acquaintance of his white bull-terrier, who because his master had had too much to drink decided to spend the night on my bed. Eric's favourite way of needling me was to say 'All *your* sex is in your voice'. I could dispute that. During the run of *Playbill* we did live television and radio versions of it; and all the theatre-world seemed to visit us.

There is little to report about a successful play: the visitors backstage, the letters, the constant discipline are taken for granted. What an audience does not know is that their presence makes just that much difference in a performance each time. The invisible wave that reaches the footlights makes actors know whether to play 'high or low' – their feeling of acceptance or antagonism can change the colour of a performance. Maybe two people in the fifteenth row of the stalls hate the whole thing; or some old lady in a box at the matinée only comes to the theatre once a year, and you play only for her; or a whisper, a laugh in the wrong place – all of it is the fibre and life or death of a performance. And this within the frame-work of what the author has said and the director demanded. I have always envied the painter, the writer, the conductor, the violinist, the dancer . . . where what they perform technically protects their nerve-ends from this very personal exposure.

A few things to remember: the evening when Queen Mary came to the play and we were summoned to the Royal Box. I had changed into the Juliet costume from *Harlequinade* in order not to hold up the intermission. Her Majesty looked at

me, puzzled: 'Were *you* that terrible woman?' Whereupon we
had a lively discussion as to what poor Millie's end might be.
Queen Mary suggested suicide. Terence Rattigan was present
to counter-argue. Another evening we were summoned to
supper with beautiful Marina, Duchess of Kent. After supper
she asked that we should play the Truth Game. Of course
no-one answered a single question truthfully.

Besides the royal visits, two other nice things: the OUDS,
Oxford, had a starry matinée, after a banquet luncheon. The
whole of *The Browning Version* was one of the items on the
programme, and while I waited I stood in the wings to watch
John Gielgud in a scene from *The Importance of Being Earnest*. It
was an exciting afternoon, and the only time I ever met or
talked to the drama critics from London; a car from the station
was shared by Mr Darlington of the *Telegraph* – who fore-
warned us all to 'speak up', but we had all heard he was
slightly deaf! The late Alan Dent sat next to me at the
luncheon and we had a lively time. I've always, if possible,
avoided meeting critics – I feel that it saves any embarrass-
ments on both sides. There are those whose opinions and
articles I would never miss – nor do I – and I wonder if the
critics realise how they can exalt or crush? I remember that in
one of my best years, a critic wrote 'Wild horses wouldn't
drag me to see her' – but he never said *why*. So for weeks I lost
all joy in my work, which had been praised by all the others, as
I raked over every aspect of it to try and find a reason for this
critic's antipathy. I can never believe the egoism that can say 'I
never pay any attention to the critics'. It just cannot be true.
About half a century later, I have come upon a lovely surprise.
Graham Greene's *Collected Film Criticisms – 1935–40* gives me
a delicious boost. It has made me feel that my Hollywood
sojourn so long ago was worthwhile, after all; and I can
remember how warming it was, after a nerve-ridden first
night, to read good things about the play and one's part in it.

Eric had film commitments, so at the end of the London

season and for the tour afterwards, Barry Jones took over. The last time we had worked together, he had been the King in *Glamorous Night* at Drury Lane, years and a war ago. He had not had a lot of luck, so *The Browning Version* fell into his hands like a ripe plum, and he gobbled it up with relish; it all ended in the early summer of 1949.

I was tired, and had pains in my neck and shoulders; I was fighting to believe that all would be well with Jock and myself. I missed him terribly. Romney Brent, who was filming in Paris, telephoned and told me to come over and forget about everything. He promised that we'd go to the opera, and drink Cassis-Vermouth at café tables; and pretend we were seeing Paris for the first time. He had always been there to talk things over with and laugh with if possible. So I went to Paris for a very hot summer week; we had supper with Yvonne Printemps and Pierre Fresnay at their little house on the outskirts. They had been in London in Noel Coward's *Conversation Piece* in 1934. She came in from the film studios, still in make-up, in a bedraggled blouse and skirt and sandals, hung with her jewels, which she took with her to the studio for safety – her dresser had to wear them all day for her, in a chamois bag under her apron. After a hard day, Yvonne insisted on singing the songs in her film for us, her magic encircling us like a scented boa-constrictor. Her two small dogs, very dirty, panting with heat, beside her on the sofa, the soda-water and whisky served warm without ice; and Pierre Fresnay, adoring, fussing about. The thing that impressed me most in their little house was a priceless fur counterpane on their huge double-bed.

We went to the opera – always a tricky experience in Paris – and saw a fine *L'Heure Espagnole* and a terrible *Jongleur de Notre Dame* in a double bill. In the *Jongleur* a fat tenor pranced in front of the Madonna in tights that threatened to split and a curly wig that fell down to his nose. But Paris was Paris, and I felt at home; and Romney, as usual, cheered me. Dinner in the

Bois – sole véronique, asparagus, and fraises du bois, window shopping, and just sitting and watching the world go by.

When I got back I was asked to do a play in September at the Edinburgh Festival: *The Man in the Raincoat* by Peter Ustinov. To be in the Festival was a lovely idea: and it meant being in Scotland, near Jock's family. This reasoning proved inconsequential; they came to the theatre enthusiastically, as they had whenever I played in Edinburgh, but it did not bring Jock any nearer. I'm sure they were as unhappy as I was about him.

Rehearsals in London were eyebrow-raising. Ustinov was marvellous – instructive, entertaining (the play not so much so), and I wouldn't have missed it for the world. We were taken by Peter to a Russian restaurant for lunches, where Bortsch and Kvass sustained us, plus the fun of hanging on to every word our histrionic director uttered. It's an adventure to be directed by him. I made one of my life-long friends in this production: Alan Wheatley, and this play would have been important to me for that reason alone.

Then, off to Edinburgh, where the red carpet was rolled out for all artists – receptions, dances, concerts. The play finishing the first week of the Festival at the Lyceum Theatre, where we were the second week's attraction, was Eliot's *The Cocktail Party*. We were able to see the closing night; the same cast played it later in London; it was superb. Our play could not match it, of course. We had a beautiful set; Alan Wheatley played a youngish judge; and George Colouris (a bit of very odd casting) was a rather Noel Coward-ish lover, returned from the past to harass the judge's wife. He certainly succeeded in harassing me, and I'm sure it was mutual. But the whole experience was delightful despite that.

On my walks, as usual, on the Royal Mile, I spotted a white alabaster hen in an antique-shop window; Alan bought it and there it was, in my dressing-room at the theatre on the opening night. I loved the old Lyceum – in the shadow of the hill and the Castle – in fact I've loved everything about Edinburgh, always. At a big party after the opening night, given I think by the Duke of Argyll, complete in kilt and ruffles, I met Rudolf Bing, the German impresario, who was director of the whole Festival. It had just been announced that he was to become Managing Director of the Metropolitan Opera House in New York. After he said the polite things about my performance, I congratulated him on his New York appointment. He said, with a German accent: 'I suppose you now wish a contract with the Metropolitan Opera House?' 'Thank you, no: I had that from 1918 to 1922.' I shall never know whether it was his joke – or whether he was really as staggered as he pretended to be. The party was fun. The whole week was festive – a pity that the play did not match it.

I had two things to work at: the BBC was doing a radio version of the Ian Hay play *Hattie Stowe*, with a huge cast, to start at the beginning of March, and a theatre play *If This Be Error* to be rehearsed in April.

I had not seen Jock to talk to for weeks, and the last session with him had left me with more understanding than hope. Now, so many years later, I know what he was seeking; I know the dream he had, and I respect his passionate social conscience that drove him to extremes. We must not forget that young people – and others – were taught to be pro-Russian during the war; indeed we were all led into that new allied loyalty, and I suppose a great many went on from there until they were totally disillusioned, as I am convinced Jock was, before the end. I am sure he suffered the double realisation of how much he had hurt his father and our marriage. I loved him – if we had only had more time!

I had started rehearsing *Hattie Stowe* for the BBC. Then, on March 6th, I had a telegram telling me Jock had been killed that morning, while testing some nylon climbing-rope on the crags outside Selkirk; he was preparing for a climbing holiday in the Alps in a few weeks' time. He had gone out very early in the morning, while no-one was about, so his body was not discovered till some hours later. The rope had broken, and he had fallen fifty feet straight onto a sharp rock which pierced his spine.

How selective is memory before it surfaces? We would live in an eternal confessional of regret and remorse and euphoria if the sub-conscious did not use a blue pencil. And how much of what is really us, interests anyone else? Especially grief. My memory doesn't lift a curtain here; there is a blank space, of recovery I suppose. Work went on into an emptiness. The most trivial things became a memorial to him: he had liked me in low heels and no make-up; this always had seemed odd to me since he had fallen in love with a different image on the Drury Lane stage. Even though I felt naked without lipstick and my feet hurt in low heels, it had pleased me to please him. Now there was no-one to please but myself, something I have never been able to do easily. It was a new low, and an arid hard patch that even music couldn't dissolve.

It passed, and the see-saw lifted me back into an unshake-able optimism that makes me – even now, at my age – wake up each morning feeling that life is still ahead of me, even though I know very well it isn't.

5

Act Two

The next thing was to manage to keep up the house. After Jock's affairs were settled I found myself with only a thousand pounds in the world; so I decided that friends would have to share my home. The basement was a perfect flat anyway. I was in luck: the play in which I found myself *If This Be Error* was not a very memorable one, even though it was produced by Kitty Black, part of the Tennent kingdom. It had Mary Morris playing my step-daughter, and Clive Morton as my husband; the jeune-premier was one Nicholas Parsons, very pink and young, just as he still looks today; and it was to open the Bath Festival before the London run. Mary Morris had a studio in Notting Hill, scheduled to be demolished. She was desperate to find a place to live, so I offered her the room leading onto the garden until she found what she wanted. There followed a most stimulating few years, until she found it. She was an amazing, talented, eccentric, and chronically compassionate young actress with a genius – whether it was for sculpting or carpentry, painting portraits of her many friends, finding treasures in flea-markets to turn into 'antiques', or giving to the first reading of a play an instinctive understanding that was more valuable than any intellectual equipment. She could be startling in Pirandello, Eugene O'Neill, or Shakespeare; or she could build a stone wall, paint a house, ski badly, but madly – she always gave an arresting performance.

I envied her abilities, and was immensely amused and interested. No-one was allowed into her room, which meant that, if I wanted to get into my garden, I had to go through the basement! She had had a very rigorous Catholic upbringing and was strangely puritanical, but with absolutely no sense of discipline or routine except in the theatre. She boasted that she never read a book, and she and my friend Raggy despaired of me and hated my orderliness which is part of my nature; I cannot help it, I was made to put things away when I was a child, and to be on time, and to be stoical about minor illnesses – all the things that seemed to irritate the two of them.

My friends gathered around in those days, to talk, and to eat. The house was alive, work abounded; but nothing could make me feel less alone. I knew I'd never want to re-marry. Impenetrable doors had closed upon an almost perfect dream; and I felt I could never risk the failure, or the ecstasy again. About this time, my mother's will was finally proven, and I found myself happily in funds.

There were evenings when Oliver Messel, Peter Ustinov and Emlyn Williams came and had coffee; Oliver giving a very funny performance as a Peruvian lady; Peter more operatic than any opera singer, and able to turn himself into a cello or a trombone; Emlyn reading aloud the lesson-book on *How to Play the Recorder* and making it unspeakably funny; and there was open house at Christmas – warmth, friendliness and happiness.

Mary Morris had a small rickety Talbot Tourer. We decided to go to the South of France to visit my cousin Paul, and Mary's Aunt Minnie who lived in Menton. The Talbot was low and shaky and turning corners on the French country roads saw me half out of it, leaning over like a trick rodeo performer. But we finally arrived in one piece. Aunt Minnie deserves a book to herself. Already in her eighties, once a singer, definitely with a colourful past, she was like a Proustian heroine, wandering around her old-fashioned, highly-polished flat, in beautiful dresses, large hats trimmed with roses, trilling bits of coloratura opera in a still perfectly pitched voice; always waiting to gamble at the Casino, or be taken to an expensive restaurant, where she demanded that a huge tip be left, in case she returned on her own one day!

She had, long years before, left her English husband and son to join an unnamed Italian aristocrat; she still wore his long military cape on occasion. With her limpid eyes growing dewy, she would tell marvellous stories of soirées in Palladian villas, where she was asked to sing. One evening she had been accompanied by Puccini. I asked what he was like. 'O ma chérie, such a little peasant.' Oh, well.

It was a great change to visit Paul in the hills just outside the old town of Vence. Paul had a very modern pre-fab studio bungalow where we listened to solid French Resistance leftist talk. His wife was his slave, and his god was Picasso, but he cooked splendidly and had a strange, probing spirit and a tenderness, mostly bestowed on his cat. Much too old for his age, completely unsophisticated, he still had mischievous, rather juvenile moments that reminded me of when we were children, and I felt a family love, if not a personal one. When I had seen him in Paris, a few years before, he had been in much more bohemian surroundings – here he seemed conventional, and patriarchal.

One morning, having coffee at a café on the Square in Vence, I saw Gordon Craig, complete in high stock, broad-brimmed black hat and cape, sitting in a corner. I went over and talked to him; it was a wonderful half hour. He told me that he had offered his private collection – I suppose of letters and designs and documents – to Britain. Either they had refused them, or been too slow in accepting them but Craig seemed distressed that France was buying them. I never got the whole story – but that morning his white hands trembled, and tears slid down his marble-hewn face, running off his nose. He died in Vence, where he had lived for years, some time later. I had been brought up to think of him as the doyen of all modern theatre design – the genius who stripped the stage of floppy canvas walls and trees and created stark beauty with his lighting. And of course he was Ellen Terry's son, and so wore a crown anyway.

When I got back from France I did a strange play by Ashley Dukes, called *Celestina*. It was set in Spain, and when we sought a guitarist to play haunting music on cue, a young man called Julian Bream presented himself and got the job. How splendid to think that even if one didn't know it then, it was one of the first engagements that our great guitarist had, sitting on a chair in the dark wings, lending moments of beauty to an otherwise rather bad play.

All through these years and months, Ivor and I had never lost each other . . . I had been interested when he asked me to come to Croydon to hear Vanessa Lee sing. Her voice was so lovely, and she herself, cool, with an untouchableness; but a kind of mad capriciousness that sometimes surfaced. She became Ivor's last leading lady and my dear friend and married Peter Graves.

Ivor and I had various meetings and suppers and talks. I went to a dress rehearsal at Covent Garden with him and, sitting next to him, felt all was not well – that odd sensing, if one loves. But he went on holiday, and I thought that was all he needed. He came back to his *King's Rhapsody* sunburned and happy. I woke up very early on March 6th 1951 and realised it was just a year to the day that Jock had been killed. The telephone rang. It was Peter Graves, telling me that Ivor had died suddenly a few hours before. Every year I dread March 6th.

I went to Paris that June for my birthday, to be run over by a bicycle opposite Weber's on the Rue Royale. The crazy French cyclist asked me to pay for his buckled front wheel and, when I came out of the restaurant later, having bathed wounded knees in brandy (of course there was no disinfectant to hand in the toilette des dames), he was still waiting, and with a policeman. I showed them my knees and asked if he wanted to pay my doctor's bill. Whereupon he and the policeman disappeared with apologies.

Paris was so lovely that June. Ice-cream at the Cascades, in the Bois, and miles of walking on the Left Bank going into dark shops. One of them I'll never forget, off the Quai d'Orsay, filled with every kind of ancient toy – paper cut-outs, model theatres; from the cup-and-ball to diavolos. And in the summer afternoons, the children shouting and playing in the gardens beside Notre Dame and in the Luxembourg. It was very unlike the Paris of my childhood. I want very much to go back again to the Quai d'Orsay now, to see Barrault's new theatre made out of that huge glass-roofed railway station: I saw him last just before the revolution of 1968 when the students demolished and desecrated his theatre.

After Paris, Norway where Helge Krog the playwright, his wife Ely and daughter Cecilie had an island off the coast. I had only been to Norway with Jock and into a world of mountaineers and skiers; this was quite the opposite – an absolute army of writers, newspapermen, and actors. The island was a granite rock covered with brambles; the house, a small wooden structure, and we each had a hut to ourselves. There were boats to sail, and to row; shrimps tickled one's legs as one swam in the smooth inlet; and in the early morning Cecilie put on huge rubber boots and scraped pails full of mussels off the briny rocks. Then one day we chugged over to another island where Mrs Krog collected every kind of mushroom, pink, yellow, orange, violet and brown. I was sure they were poison, but the great pot that evening held the most luscious dish; even if the coffee had been re-boiling all day, great gulps of Aquavit cancelled any ill effects. Then to Sweden and Stockholm, ending up in Denmark; and Copenhagen, one of my favourite cities. Then back to London in a sick-making North Sea storm.

54 &55 Eric Portman and myself in our two *Playbill* roles as Millie and Andrew Crocker-Harris in *The Browning Version* and Edna Selby and Arthur Gosport in *Harlequinade*

56 Outside the dressing rooms at the Stratford Memorial Theatre, 1952

It was September, and the moment I got home I was asked
to do the 1952 Stratford-upon-Avon season. Rehearsals
started in January for a March opening. It meant being in
Stratford for nine months. Glen Byam Shaw and Anthony
Quayle took me to an expensive lunch in the Carlton Grill; I
hadn't played in Shakespeare since *The Taming of the Shrew* in
1927, and that day I shed tears into my Dover sole, trying to
refuse because I wanted so much to do it, and do it well, and
wasn't sure I could. They finally persuaded me that I should
play Volumnia in *Coriolanus*. It was to open the new season.
So I decided to enjoy it and turned to the soaring words.

                    *   *   *

Stratford-upon-Avon in 1952 – the year that George VI died,
Elizabeth II became Queen, and I had to play Volumnia. A
loneliness beyond belief in the Arden Hotel. Rehearsing
all day, and then everyone disappearing to their rooms or
cottages or digs. Very cold – awful food; an icy fog along the
Avon, where even the swans seemed frozen. The theatre itself
forbidding. Me, frightened out of my wits; I felt I was being
thrown to the Shakespearean lions. But gradually there was
a slight thaw and a gleam of friendliness and laughter
and warmth: Siobhan McKenna, Laurence Harvey, Michael
Hordern . . . Anthony Quayle himself much too busy with
family and theatre and the role of Coriolanus to be able to
bother about anyone or anything; and Glen Byam Shaw,
directing; Jack Wilson's studio where all the exotic props and
head-dresses were made so beautifully, and Denne Gilkes'
home on the High Street where the younger fry gathered.
Denne taught voice production and singing. She was a large,
smock-dressed woman, with a grey page-boy haircut, looking rather like an un-Jewish edition of G.B. Stern. The house
was full of cats giving birth and young people giving voice.
    The pub was The Dirty Duck where, after the morning
rehearsal, everyone foregathered. But for weeks I was too shy,

and crept off silently to those awful cold-platter lunches in the hotel, and at night, still colder, into a rather institutional bedroom. The atmosphere cleared a bit after the opening, in March, and friends started coming to Stratford to spend the weekends with me. Ralph Richardson came to play Prospero; Margaret Leighton, Ariel. Gossip was rife. Laurence Harvey, young and blazing with Slav virility as Aufidius in *Coriolanus*, swooning over Miss Leighton who arrived for her daily re-hearsals on her bicycle, looking as fresh as the early daffodils. But Laurence Harvey had swooned over Siobhan too . . .

I was in no swooning mood, so made friends with the younger element: Michael Bates and sweet Maggie Chisholm whom he later married; Brendan Barry, who looked like a Polynesian warrior and had a most glorious Welsh bass voice, deep beyond his years. Later I arranged for him to study with Frank Titterton who believed he should go into opera. But Barry had to keep working to exist, and so missed his chance, as so many young talents do; there was Teddy Atienza too, who played the guitar and sang lovely folk-songs. And they were all almost young enough to be my children.

Mary Morris was busy with *The Young Elizabeth* in London, a lucky play to be in as our own Elizabeth became Queen. It was at the Criterion Theatre, where Yvonne Arnaud had just finished a play, and in the Star dressing-room Mary said she kept finding remains of cream cakes stuffed down the upholstery, reminders of the inimitable Miss Arnaud's indulgences, and opulent waistline.

That summer everyone seemed to come to Stratford for a visit. University professors from the United States and bus-loads of tourists; there were lunches with actor friends; gossip, stories of the past seasons, interviews, photographers; Shakespeare's birthday celebrations; watching John Gielgud directing – a lean arrow in a black turtle-neck sweater; having lunch with Margaret Leighton and wondering how she could play her lovely Rosalind eating nothing but a lettuce leaf and lemon juice; seeing Siobhan get deliciously dizzy on red wine at an after-theatre party and walking home in the moonlight singing after a big party towards the end of the season. None of us will ever forget that party. Uninvited guests appeared, and a big Stilton cheese disappeared (a note came later from Michael Hordern, explaining); and we rollicked and made music until the dawn broke. And always, home to London whenever I could.

I learned a lot that season. And in the months that followed, even more. Television kept me busy. Then one evening a telephone call came from Noel Coward. I had known him, of course, and admired his very special gifts unreservedly. In the Ivor days I had felt their love-hate attitude towards one another and, as Ivor's chief protagonist, I had been in the line of battle. I had long since sworn I would not sing again and Noel knew I had not done so for years. But I was amused, and excited, when he asked me to play Mrs Erlynne in *After the Ball*, his musical version of *Lady Windermere's Fan*, and I felt I could manage his songs – and looked forward to working for him tremendously. Alas, from the beginning, we could not get onto the same wavelength. For some reason he gave me the most overpowering sense of inferiority. Never a very confident person, at beginning of rehearsals, I was thrown into the depths by a word or a grimace or a dash of his heavy sarcasm – perhaps just because I so much wanted to please him.

In Brighton at a final rehearsal, after a stampede of corrections and changes and cuts, I ran off to my dressing-room in order to save myself from breaking down on the stage. Noel followed, furiously keeping up the barrage; so I asked him why, if he felt I wasn't right for the part, had he not let me go before – and even now? He said that if he could find someone else he certainly would. After a night of feeling suicidal something exploded, and everything in me went cold and clear and uncaring and determined. I will never know the why or wherefore of it all; it seems ridiculous now that, with years of theatre behind me, I found myself in this most humiliating adventure. It wasn't the fault of either of us. I think it all started this way: I am a very small person, but look much taller on the stage. When we first discussed the casting, Noel had suggested Joyce Redmond as Lady Windermere, but this was forgotten and I found myself towered over by two of the tallest people on the stage as Lord and Lady Windermere: so much so, that I relished the critic who said in his review in Cardiff (where we were 'trying out' before London): 'Why did Miss Ellis make her entrance on her knees?' It made me feel like a female Toulouse-Lautrec.

After the Ball opened at the Globe, and pleased many people very much, but I never sang another note. 'The Master' had done his work well. It is interesting that whenever we met afterwards, or wrote, it was with affection. Years later I remember specially a lovely day spent with him in his house in Switzerland. And once, an episode which was great fun. One night while he was filming his *Astonished Heart* he telephoned me to ask me to play one scene in it, to learn it overnight: he would send the script within the hour and I must be at Pinewood word perfect the next morning. I said of course I'd do it, but asked not to be put on the cast-list. The studio session was marvellous; and to this day people who see the film telephone me to say: 'There's a woman in the doctor's office scene who looks exactly like you!'

No matter how much he hurt me, I know now it was because I had not the gristle in me to take it, and I'm sure I benefited. I'd been so protected and spoiled in the theatre – and his was that ruthless world that sought perfection in almost brutal ways. And we were really very fond one another!

Katherine Hepburn arrived in Cardiff for the first performance of *After the Ball*; she was a great friend of Robert Helpmann who was directing the opus. She was marvellous, and gave us all an after-theatre supper at a restaurant down by the docks. I had been resting that afternoon when I heard her unmistakeable voice chatting in the hotel room next to mine. I thought I was having pre-performance delirium, but it was the peerless Katy, who graced her supper-party in a Cardinal-like cloak and cheered us inordinately.

Other nice things happened during the run. The Duchess of Kent, Marina, and a very shy Princess Alexandra came to my dressing-room after a performance, both so beautiful; and Marlene Dietrich, Noel's great friend (I hadn't seen her since Hollywood) came another night in a skin-tight white dress with her Légion d'Honneur, I think it was, like a bright red drop on her bosom.

My thoughts go back to the closing week of *After the Ball* in Blackpool, New Year, 1955. We had had a short provincial tour, to finish it off. A Blackpool hotel on New Year's Eve is something rather terrifying: noise and paper streamers and balloons; stomachy, unsteady gentlemen, wandering in the halls; their stout wives waiting for them in over-stuffed moquette lounge chairs; New Year's Eve supper, after the play, of over-cooked turkey in pale oxo gravy and ice-cream in dented metal goblets. Devastatingly the contradiction of any star-ritual. Thoroughly depressed, I was revived in London by the Arts Theatre wanting me to play in the O'Neill play *Mourning Becomes Electra* to be directed by Peter Hall, fresh from his first great success, *Waiting for Godot*. All was right with the world again. It was another marathon, like *Strange Interlude* which had been my first introduction to London, twenty-three years before.

A voyage back to New York to see my sister had already been arranged for the week after the Coward play closed. I hadn't seen her, and my nieces and nephews since Mother's death nine years before, and I wanted to take Mary Morris with me, to show her New York. Her family had been so kind to me, and I hoped mine would be to her. I needn't have worried about that. They fell for her, solidly, with affectionate and amused thuds of approval.

New York was safe and vastly exciting in those pre-mugging days. After a short stay, we went down to Nassau in the Bahamas to spend a week with Romney Brent, who was playing Shaw's *Don Juan in Hell* in the winter season there. Anything less likely to attract sun-baked audiences I can't imagine. The sea was warm, but the wind cold; the black population sullen and antagonistic; I suppose in the upper reaches of hotels and villas and yachts this went unnoticed; whether it was there, or in the Greek Islands, or the South of France, the cocoon was the same – the tycoons, the extra-marital blondes . . . the caviar was as salty, the drinks as paralysing. And a rebellious group of natives was always watching and waiting. I understood their sullen and frightening silence.

Then back to New York, and to my sister in her lovely Connecticut 'salt-box' house – in the New England countryside of granite and birch-trees, snow, chipmunks, and high skies. It was strange to be with her: we knew each other so little; but blood proved much thicker than the long braid of her still gorgeous Titian hair; and the years between started to vanish. I think she is the most honest person I know, in her approach to everyone, including herself. She had chosen her ivory tower, and it never occurred to her to leave it, even to visit me. With her painter husband Arthur Emptage, she watched the world go by, much 'bewildered' – her favourite word.

Ever since then, wherever I have lived, I have hopefully kept rooms for my sister to come to – but she has never left her Connecticut retreat. As I write this, she is ninety, frail and ill; still not wanting to be part of the world as it is – and ready to leave it.

I was amazed to find myself so completely detached from New York. I had expected to feel something; the only moment of stabbing memory was when I stood opposite the yellow façade of the Old Metropolitan Opera House, now in the sleaziest part of town – littered, dusty, dirty; down-and-outs leaning in doorways, shabby women with swollen ankles and huge parcels, waddling in and out of the pushing, un-caring, lunch-bound office-workers; sirens of ambulances and cars; screeches of brakes. Then, for a split second the street in front of me emptied and from somewhere a shiny black limousine drew up, and a jaunty, panama-hatted man got out followed by a group of men, looking like the Mafia; the stage-door man bowed, 'Good morning, Mr Caruso'. . . then the iron safety curtain of the past came down with a bang.

We returned from New York to start rehearsing *Mourning Becomes Electra* on May 1st. It had not been seen in London since 1937. I found it a less interesting play than *Strange Interlude*; perhaps because it was built on the borrowed bones of the Greek tragedy. But it was inspiring. Peter Hall was a remarkable young man and a vital director. I remember only one argument and that was over the idea of the porch which was the key and scene of so much action; the English designer had thought of it in terms of the ordinary suburban house; in the New England tradition, and according to O'Neill and Robert Edmond Jones, who first designed the production, it had to be the Greek pillared façade of a typical New England colonial house. It was settled by my sending a cable to the Theatre Guild for the photographs of the original production, and we had a splendid setting. I love to think that I was directed by Peter in his second London production. The first had been *Waiting for Godot*. One day, getting out of a taxi at the National Theatre, to see *The Country Wife*, I came face to face with him – now of course Sir Peter Hall, with the great responsibility of our National Theatre in all its varying and controversial splendour – he looked down at me from his bearded height with an astonished dawning recognition; I wonder if he remembered it all?

Ronald Lewis, John Phillips, Joseph O'Connor, Mary Morris and myself. . . It literally was blood and sweat, for the summer weeks were swelteringly hot – Victorian costumes heavy, and the play lasting for four hours. But audiences were superb, and we had double the usual run at the Arts Theatre. I felt at ease with the O'Neill words, a sort of back to the womb feeling that I had lost for America itself. I find I often get a nostalgia for places, through words . . . except for Paris, which comes to me when I smell wet pavements in the sun, freshly ground coffee, baking bread, and violets. London seems free of sounds, with a special grey-gold light that matches the Nash Terraces and even seeps into the grimy brick of the East End.

I can't understand why I did not play in the theatre again until 1959. There were television plays galore, radio pro- grammes in London and New York, even a first colour tele- vision version of Henry James' *The Tutor* made at the old film studios in Brooklyn. I am appalled to read in a diary that I turned down *The Elder Statesman* by T.S. Eliot, offered to me by Henry Sherek, a part I should have given my eye-teeth to play. There was a lot of travelling and two or three journeys to the United States. But I remember best visiting Jean Louis Barrault in Paris, where he was producing Claudel's *Tête d'Or*, and then driving along miles of wheatfields near Orleans; and the hushed cool darkness of Chartres Cathedral, the famous rose window lighting it like a subdued heavenly sun; Les Landes, a flat untrammelled part of France full of pines and lakes, looking like the perfect setting for Chekhov's *Three Sisters*, leading down towards Bordeaux; and a visit to Lourdes, horrifying in its commercial holiness. The green glinting copper rocks of the southern gorges, and a little mountain village on the Route Napoléon where there is an inn called Fifi Moulin.

*   *   *

In London I seemed to be commuting to the television studios. Unfortunately for me – because I'd love to see them again – this was all done live, before the plays were taped.

57 With Vanessa Lee in Noël Coward's *After the Ball*, Globe Theatre, London, 1954

58 With John Phillips in Peter Hall's production of Eugene
O'Neill's *Mourning Becomes Electra*, Arts Theatre, London, 1955

59 My last West End appearance in *Look Homeward, Angel* with
Peter McEnery, Phoenix Theatre, London, 1962

60 My last stage appearance in Bernard Shaw's *Mrs Warren's
Profession*, Yvonne Arnaud Theatre, Guildford, 1970

When there was a suggestion that I should do a play, *The Rose Tattoo* by Tennessee Williams, I rushed to Copenhagen for the weekend, where it was being done in an art theatre. The Danish version smacked more of salt-fish than Coca-Cola and spaghetti, but as a side-issue I saw one of the best *Madame Butterfly*'s at the Opera – a little Finnish soprano perfect as Cio-Cio-San, and a great blond Swedish tenor as Pinkerton. All of Copenhagen enchanted me: the Danish ladies in frilly blouses and flowery hats, eating cream cakes at ten in the morning and smoking cigars; the Tivoli Gardens with its glass concert hall; the smiling good humour of everyone from the Fishmarket to the Palace guards, and the language which sounds like a staccato scale of muted horns.

I started writing again, and sending stories to magazines, and got out the paint-brushes too; but I missed the theatre terribly. Each evening at about six I felt lost. It was the hour to start thinking about the performance and the audience. Londoners were going home after work: this was the time actors started their living, and every actor knows how the evenings, jobless, become an aching void. It had to be got over.

In December 1955, I needed someone to help and cook in the over-big house. One day a little woman from Grenada, in the West Indies, came to be interviewed. She was dressed in grey and sat on the edge of the sofa holding her umbrella, answering questions softly – a quarter of a century ago: she has been with me ever since, hardly changed at all, devoted and efficient; her intuition has helped me many times and her good sense too. She can make any plant grow – I have heard her talking to stubborn things in their pots, growing in a South of France garden, or in my kitchen in London. One night in France she waited with me, in the garden there, with a torch to watch the once-a-summer midnight blooming cactus burst like a star; and whenever she planted a peach-stone, or a cutting, the reward came. Besides all this, she bears the

magical name of Lyris, which sounds to me like some forgotten Muse . . . and is very much at odds with her practical
self.

Of course, a play came out of the blue: about a Christian
Science teacher, written by an American, and called *Dark
Halo*. Clifford Williams was asked to direct it, not well-
known as yet: he came to see me off at the BOAC terminal
when I had to go to New York to see the authoress; and after a
hectic visit there, giving her his suggestions for changes, I
hurried back and was thrilled to be in harness again and
working with Williams and a cast that proved to be better than
the play. The main character was based on Mary Baker Eddy.
In its 'God is love' way it was strangely atheistic. It frightened
me a bit and was too dangerous a play for the commercial
theatre. Since then I've watched Clifford Williams soar to
directorial heights and admire him very much.

Then came an offer to go to Spain to do a film, *The Three
Worlds of Gulliver*. Columbia asked me to play the Queen of
Lilliput, but I read the script and found the Giant Queen of
Brobdingnag much more amusing, so they switched me to
that. Basil Sydney was playing the King of Lilliput, and I did
not really delight in the idea of acting his Queen . . . Gregoire
Aslan was the King of Brobdingnag and Gulliver was played
by Kerwin Matthews. Matt and I were the only ones to
survive the heat without the usual Spanish stomach ache; we
lived on yoghourt and orange juice in the studio, while the nice
American director courted death with steaks and ice-creams.

Madrid fascinated and horrified me. I was put into a
modern luxury hotel; my room overlooked the garden of a
convent and I could see the nuns feeding their chickens and
laughing at their antics; the room waiter, who brought my
breakfast, cheerfully taught me two or three Spanish words
each day and, as work at the studios didn't even start till
eleven, I had plenty of time to walk and explore. The shops
were beautiful: in their windows, perhaps, one great yellow

diamond on a blue velvet cushion, or a single pair of hand-made shoes, flood-lit; behind the main street, filthy stark poverty, beggars, ragged children. One old crone pushed me in the ribs and, grinning, opened her coat to show rows of wrist-watches and fountain pens hung on its lining. I got used to these morning discoveries.

The Prado was gorgeous: all the Velasquez and Goya magnificence, beautifully hung; I spent many free hours there. On another day I took a bus to Toledo; miles of road across acres of dry barren yellow earth, speared with black trees, and an occasional mule-pulled plough. Toledo, truly golden: the river running gold beneath the cliffs and old buildings; the young boys beating gold into the ebony sword-handles and jewellery in the factories; crooked streets of gold coloured stone leading to El Greco's house where his twelve myopic paintings of the Apostles looked warily at the tourists. In Madrid, after filming all day, ice-cold gaspacho at eleven o'clock suppers in the hotel – spontaneous Flamencos being danced in the Square – as well as perfectly rehearsed ones in the night clubs; those immaculate small bottoms of the stamping males and lush petticoats and bosoms and banshee vocal allure of the girls. It was all over too soon. But I had been able to save a lot of money. And apart from all that, I had seen my only bull-fight. We had to go, for some publicity reason; but no reasoning could condone the sick-making spectacle; the matadors like ballet-dancers, the young bull, foaming, pawing, blowing; the savage yells of the crowd, the gored toreador, and a smell of blood; the tired, starved horses, and more than anything, that poor black beast falling to his knees with a dozen ribboned darts in his shoulders. I had been curious about bull-fights ever since one afternoon in Aix-en-Provence: we had only been able to get in at a hotel called Le Mule Noir – a place where the bull-fighters stayed. On the way to my room, I passed an open door; a huge bed, with a pair of black velvet trousers and a long red sash thrown on its gilded posts; I could only see the white-stockinged feet of the wounded toreador lying there . . . several men, crowding around, hushed and still, and a doctor pushing past me in the hallway and into the room. It was like *Death in the Afternoon*. The tiles and floor shone in the shafts of a setting sun. Everything was very white and red and black; and dry and noisy.

Ten years later, in 1971, I was in Aix-en-Provence for a music festival. Open air productions of *Pelléas et Mélisande* and *Falstaff*, performed in the courtyard of the Arch-Veque's Palace (that courtyard with its music again!), and afterwards walking back in the moonlight, with Romney, who was visiting me that summer, was like being transferred to a world of medieval beauty. Incidentally, it was the best production of *Pelléas* that I've ever seen, despite a mistral-wind which blew up furiously half-way through, and sent people scurrying to buy shawls and rugs in the intermission at the stalls suddenly opened around the Square, prepared for just such emergencies – trust the French!

The heat and sun must have driven me to dream of the Alps again. I had been thinking of finding some mountain to perch on during my holidays. A chalet, very small, in the meadows facing the Dents du Midi and a deep-distant view of the tail-end of Lac Leman, was the answer for several years. Mary Morris had bought a Land-rover and she and David Dennis helped to bring over bits and pieces, and to scrape the wood down to its original white pine, and to paint and plaster. David now has his own haven on a hilltop village in Italy, and Mary has built herself a fantastic place out of a five hundred year old cow-shed in Switzerland; but then we were content and excited to make that house, which looked like a Swiss music-box, as liveable as possible. At any season it was lovely: even in ten days of dense mountain fog, when David said it might as well be called 'Sea-View', and even when I was alone there one fortnight, digging myself out of eight feet of snow, and getting water in buckets from a pipe line in the forest on a child's sled, because all the mains were frozen. In the summers all the gentians and violas and anemones made the meadows look like stained glass church windows, and there was a herd of biscuit-coloured cows that absolutely danced down the hill, bells clanging, when they were let out of their huts at sunset. They were very friendly, clean cows, who allowed the indignity of having their backsides hosed every night.

All my friends came, often; except Romney, who was touring all over the world with Helen Hayes for the Theatre Guild – and Romney hated Switzerland anyway; he said it only made clocks and cheeses, and was too clean. I understood his feelings better when a few years later I visited him in Mexico!

During times spent longing for the theatre, when one's mummer's spirit is at its lowest, something good often happens. After more television plays, *The Voice of the Turtle* in the first Maugham series and *Strangers in a Room* for Manchester and a radio play or two, it was exciting to be asked to do *Look Homeward Angel*, a play made from Thomas Wolfe's great novel. I suppose the younger son was Wolfe himself, and the woman I played a deeply observed character study of his amazing mother, who owned a boarding house and battled with her sons and her idealistic husband, who sculpted tombstones. The play was to be done at Croydon where the theatre was in the Round. I had met Richard Pasco in the Manchester television studios and persuaded him to play the eldest son in *Homeward Angel*. Peter McEnery was to be the younger son. These two actors, so young at that time, have never looked back. I try to see everything Richard Pasco does. He is now one of the leading actors of the Royal Shakespeare Company. There is something very compelling and touching in all his work and his gorgeous sense of humour rides high.

Andrew Cruickshank was the great old man; Terence Kilburn directed. Acting in the Round was inspiring, and I think the play lost something when it transferred to the

Phoenix Theatre in 1963. It was very American in its intellectual approach to passions and mores – an inhibiting and
general fault, I feel, with most thinking modern Americans,
who seem to forget that the basis of simple emotions can be
made difficult when dealt with in their eternal idiom of psy-
chiatry, which at its worst can make even a sneeze or hang-nail
a reason for confusion. This perpetual self-analysis and seeking for hidden motive is all the sadder because by nature they
are such a forthright and ingenuous people.

On my holidays I gradually realised that being on my own
at the chalet was depressing; and the cutting down of forests in
the valley to make way for an oil refinery let the mists and fogs
from the lake sweep up to me and my bronchial tubes. The
mountains were very different without Jock – it was no use
trying to relate to them completely again, even if I always
went back to them. So of course, I thought of the sun and the
south again. It is so much easier to be alone in a warm climate.

One day at the chalet, when Mary Morris returned from
ski-ing, she said she had talked to an English woman who had
invited us to her chalet in Villars for drinks the next evening.
She was Queen Bee of the ski-ing world at Villars. As I was
not in the least 'sportive', I wasn't impressed; but it was she
who gave me excellent advice when I decided to build The
Cansoun in St Paul in 1966, in the hills above Nice. With the
blessing of the Bank of England I was allowed a holiday home
in France. I had hoped to find an old farmhouse and renovate
it; but instead bought some land and found a local Provençal
builder who, with ancient tiles and beams collected from
demolished farms and the great stones turned up by the bull-
dozer on two acres of hillside, managed to follow my fantasies
scribbled on bits of paper and create a lovely house, which
looked almost as though it had been on that hill for centuries.
My ski-ing friend from Villars, who knew the French idio-
syncracies well, could tell when to scold, or give a bottle of
wine; result – it was built in a year. As she had worked for the

Free French during the war, she managed to get a telephone installed by a correspondence with de Gaulle himself, which episode brought her the trembling respect of the Mayor of St Paul and the awed curiosity of the road engineers putting in the new telephone wires. It was like a Jacques Tati film.

Mimosa, cypress, and figs grew wild. My neighbour was a Polish communist, who grew superb carnations for the Nice market; above me on the hill lived a famous old Spiritualist, a Mrs Garrett, who when I moved in sent me sheaves of gladioli from her greenhouses. These flowers, in their spiky, hard, unscented way, have always seemed devilish to me; they reminded me of Mephistopheles in *Faust* with his pointed cap and cape-collar. There was a swimming-pool, too, perilously hung onto the hill and, later, a pavilion guest house below, built for the overflow of friends, and where Lyris helped the vegetable garden to flourish. I finally moved in during a storm-tossed autumn, and from then on the work was un-ending. I refused to make it my permanent home because Britain was where I worked and belonged: I have the old-fashioned idea that the country where you work and get paid should collect the taxes. So despite well-wishing advice I never was a 'tax-exile', and am the poorer but happier for it. Besides, where else except in London could you hear and see every great artist and orchestra perform, see the best in the theatre, and opera and ballet – the exhibitions of Bonnard, Magritte, Fabergé, the gold of Egypt, Moore, Hepworth, and all those between, below and above, where queues a mile long wait for all this, and in all weathers? I don't think people in London realise or appreciate enough their freedom and im-mense opportunities. Even the television is the best in the world – and so are the taxi-drivers.

The years at the Cansoun – that word means song, in Provençal, pronounced with a gutteral twang – did not turn out as I had dreamed. I had so wanted the place to be some-where where everyone I loved could come and do exactly as they liked, forget their troubles and rest and swim and sun themselves, play music till dawn if they wished, talk and laugh, visit the wonderful Maeght Museum on the high hill, have an out-of-this-world meal occasionally at the Mas-des-Serres, and explore the hills around. I had wanted this so much, since my first glimpse of St Paul with Tim, in 1937. Despite the visits from Alan and Romney, Tim, Vanessa and Peter, and my niece, my cousin Paul who lived nearby in Vence in his messy studio – and later Michael O'Shaughnessy who painted in a mouldering old lodge with a tangled garden; despite the sunsets, and the unbelievable experience of looking up at a clear, shining moon at the same moment that the television on the table was showing a man stepping onto it for the first time; despite the Brown Owl who left feathers for me on the terrace, and the din of the mating frogs around the pool, and the chattering of the house-swifts in spring; the early marketing at Vence, the over-size prawns, the frightening view of forest-fires across the valley – despite everything, it did not add up . . . Every year, new villas grew like mushrooms on the landscape. It was no longer peaceful. But I grew to love the people around: and found them very different from the money-minded northern French. When I came back to my flat in London, and the iron-grey winter, I managed to put some of it down on canvas, and I can warm myself now, looking at what I painted, even though the Cansoun has long since been sold.

It was hard to be busy enough; but a revival of *The Silver Cord* (by Sidney Howard) in 1970 – that terrifying study of a possessive mother – came along, to be played at Guildford's theatre, the Yvonne Arnaud. I enjoyed myself there, visiting the University, and having the unique experience of being offered Mao's *Little Red Book*, for sale on the street outside Marks & Spencer's. Romney came to spend a lot of the summer with me, and we had enough theatre talk to fill me up for a while. Then, Margaret Webster, the director of so much

Shakespeare in America and of some unforgettable opera productions, came back to England. I had met her, Peggy, when we were both at our beginnings, at her mother and father's house: Dame May Whitty and Ben Webster were two of the first to welcome me to London in 1932 and in their rather Dickensian flat I was impressed with a new central heating system – a copper pipe running around the floor wainscotting, very new for London. I had been used to steam heat and shivered in the back-biting draughts of doors with those large upholstered sausages at their cracks. When, fifty years later, Peggy Webster said she wanted to direct Bernard Shaw's *Mrs Warren's Profession* in 1970 at Guildford for me, of course I was delighted. And we had high hopes of it being transferred to London, not realising that a revival was on the way for the same season at the National Theatre. Susannah York, Alan Wheatley and Clive Morton were in it too – Susannah an extraordinary and lovable actress, already a film-star but unspoiled by that, eager and warm. It was wonderful to work for Peggy. Not one of us suspected that she was ill, and it was a great shock, some time later, to know she had been suffering courageously and travelling to and fro between London and the United States, seeing her friends and working at another book, right up to the last. She left us all with a lesson in courage and perception and gentleness, in league with her great talents.

New York at Christmas – and my first visit to The Lincoln Center, and the New Metropolitan Opera House. What impressed me more than all the Chagall murals and Viennese chandeliers was the fact that a tube train – the subway – ran right into the huge basement of the Opera House, so that on this snowy night of *Meistersinger* Romney and I were able to get from his flat into the Opera House without transport worries. The train coming back was like a festival bus, everyone carrying the programmes, getting off at all stations between the Met. and Greenwich Village – really a super idea.

We had a lovely party afterwards where Lillian Gish, as exquisite as ever, was chief guest. Everyone loved coming to Romney's in the Spanish quarter of downtown. I think he was loved by more people than anyone I know, and the next year I finally visited him in Mexico, where he had been born, and where he died soon after. He lived in the centre of Mexico City in a balconied flat, filled with music, his father's medals and swords, books, and two bathrooms the size of ballrooms; and on his balconies lovely plants of the forbidden cannabis, used in Mexico chiefly for decoration and to make a liniment for rheumatism. It was Easter time and the church doors were open day and night, a thousand candles burning. The city dripped with gold and silver, and with mountains of fruit in the markets. Taxis were shared and a peasant with a live white goose tucked under his arm, looking like the cartoons of sleepy Mexicans, sombrero and all, climbed into the front seat one day and wished me good health. These two levels all through: the black sweaty braids and expensive hair-do's; the sky-scrapers, hovels and Cathedrals; terrorists and extreme wealth; and the deep Aztec roots that were overwhelming.

Peacocks in gardens, ancient excavations surrounded by workers' flats; Popocatapetl, snow-crested, and the hill-people surrounded by goats and herbs; a theatre with a huge mosaic eye over the portico, where Dolores del Rio still can command an adoring audience; in the Park the most wonderful archaeological museum in the world; and a restaurant under a roof of glass, on the edge of a lake, where promptly at ten o'clock the fountains burst into floods of light. On Sundays the Park was crowded with country folk in bright pinks and yellows, the children holding paper toys, as intricately designed as the little Madonnas for sale in every shop; a baroque yellowing Opera House, and the most amazing vast new underground, to equal the one in Moscow.

Cuernavaca, where we visited Bob Brady – his guest-book filled with famous names from Rebecca West down; his house like a museum; his hosting perfect. I'd love to go back, but Romney is dead, and there would be no laughter.

Flying back to New York, in a small Mexican plane, the pilot swooped low over the golden pyramids. A wonder of thought-out beauty thousands of years ago, making the present seem synthetic; and when we arrived, the concrete and glass of New York looked unimposing to me for the first time.

One day a couple of years ago, I set out on an American adventure. Alan came with me – I would not have done it without him. There is a favourite academic American pastime: the Universities ask authors, actors, and almost anyone who has a thought-provoking subject, to talk to them; give a lecture, partake in a forum, answer questions, and either be made to feel foolish or heroic in the process – all for a modest fee. I had resisted any temptation from the heads of drama departments, but when my nephew, the gentlest and most lovably intelligent of men who runs just such a forum in New England near a University, suggested a theatre weekend of three talks and readings of plays, Alan and I got our tickets, packed our bags, got ourselves into the mood of Shakespeare, Shaw, Pinter and Coward; and I prepared a paper on the history of the theatre, beginning with Thespis the Greek who had a cart and horse that stopped in market places, so that he could recite epics.

We had a gorgeous time, and the place itself was a heartening experience. The hills are wide and beautiful with no house in sight: summer symphony concerts a few miles away; folk museums, a Shaker village; the Francis Clarke Museum which surprisingly houses over a hundred Renoir paintings; and the villages where houses stand white among birch and pine and where the farmhouses make that astringent ambrosia, syrup and sugar tapped from the maple trees.

This New England has its Puritan links with the past, and some left-over Georgian splendour too, and the hidden totems of the Red Indians whose spirits haunt the dogwood and give their names to the rivers and lakes and mountains. I get an 'ethnic' sensation when I think about it.

To travel with Alan Wheatley is to risk his being instantly recognised as the Sheriff of Nottingham because that old *Robin Hood* television film still goes on all over the world. Whether by a group of children on a small bridge over an Alpine stream or this time, by the gentleman taking boarding-cards at the Boston airport, it's 'Hiya, Sheriff!' to the delight of my family, and the startled curiosity of the other passengers.

The biggest 'putting in one's place' is in the Lincoln Center's Theatre Library. There, actors, directors, singers, musicians, all of us who have had to do with the theatre from all over the world are reduced to yellow cards – years and years of us – just great files of photographs, letters, notices . . . I thought I was going to see a collection of glowing, astonishing memorabilia; instead there were huge library tables, over-hung with green reading-lamps; empty corridors, and grey metal files, files, files – something out of computer-science fiction. You can ask about some great actress of the past and a man in shirtsleeves dumps a sheaf of cardboard cards in your lap. I hope so much that when finally our Theatre Museum is established in London it will have all the colour and warmth – excitement and humanity – that the most gallant and generous profession deserves.

Back home where, after the tussles with those over-alert and enquiring minds in the United States, the plainest of British folk seemed to wear their insignificance with distinction. America is still so young! And when you get past the tight shackles of big business and stress, they are not very different from their original pioneering selves that hunted gold in the West.

Another Beginning

It's Easter-time; the 1980s – a spell of absolutely schizophrenic weather has unbalanced the glands and mind. That, plus the seeming complete madness of the world, gives one a sense of living in a kind of suspended vacuum; it's only the emergence of a new generation just out of the egg that seems to have vestiges of sense and imagination clinging to it like bits of shell; I hope I live long enough to see what happens. The nearer the past comes to the present, the more difficult I find it to be objective.

Recently at the Festival Hall I heard Perlman and Ashkenazy playing three Beethoven sonatas. I think the hall is too big for these but, even so, it was near perfection. Then there was the recent recital by Gidon Kremer; he played his violin for two hours, without even the piano to support him, miraculous; he has only been allowed out of Russia to visit here for a concert or two. He is thirty and looks like an old print caricature of Paganini, his thin spindly legs like a spider's, his violin a fifth limb; he is all music. The packed hall rose to its feet with a roar; it seems only music and sometimes ballet can make an audience react this way now. Maybe because they recognise complete dedication in this diffusive age? Anyway, it's heartening to sit spell-bound and feel the same electric one-ness that I used to feel from the other side of the foot-lights, as if I could embrace the audience and know them all; a kind of replete strength, as much accepting as giving.

Full circle, finally, from hiding under the piano while my mother played, or throwing pennies down to vagrant musicians from a nursery window. I must learn now to be the consumer, not the worker. Yet the absolute lust to work persists. Why, or how, or for what, I'll never know. I have missed the actual physical exaltation of singing, and I miss going to the opera. Time was, when I heard *Rosenkavalier* whenever I could, as much for the von Hoffmansthal libretto as the Strauss music; *Eugene Onegin; Meistersinger*; the Puccinis, Verdis, and all of Mozart, whenever and wherever possible (and sometimes in very strange places). Now it is all such a struggle to get there, to buy tickets, to get transport. And having bought an outrageously expensive seat, the smell of wet woollens, old leather and unwashed hair is apt to be beside you or in front of you. It shouldn't matter I know, but oh! for the gala nights of perfume wafted by fanning programmes, the buzz of discussion between acts, the delighted hush and expectancy . . . I think television has cancelled all that. Perhaps I am wrong and sadly old-fashioned to think it is important; but the lack of it is something that strikes deep into this concrete and chrome age; there is no baroquery, no conscious graciousness, just the bare fact of performances to be accepted or not.

Anyway, to be at the theatre is always an excitement for me. I have never left before a play was over, even if I see all the wheels working, or even if it's tawdry, or dreary, or a disaster. I will brave wind and weather to see Paul Scofield in anything. I watch the young greats full of expectation; and there are so many young actors on the fringe of possible greatness – more than ever before.

Why did I ever imagine I'd have time to do everything I meant to, see everything, hear everything? Now as the years pile on and go faster and faster, I feel like Alice who asked the Red Queen why they were running. 'To stay in the same place, of course', the Red Queen said.

Sometimes it seems to me that the only Romantics left are the great conductors and directors of theatre and films. Theirs is still an expected dictatorship; they are allowed their style, their eccentricities. Not so long ago, the individual artist was excused his temperament, his oddities, and the public forgave and worshipped. Whether for better or worse, now, it's the group, the team, the Company that matters. Only when one sees Fonteyn dance, hears Pollini at the piano or perhaps Janet Baker singing Berlioz's 'Nuits d'Éte', or Fischer-Dieskau translating Schubert into a universal language, or even some of those uninhibited star performances in French films and, of course, our well-seasoned British actors, does one realise a world lost. But the world has discovered a new kind of vitality – it makes up for that loss somewhat in a tremendous insistence of communication, which is what must save us from extinction. This process, as theatre life fades for me, is a paradox anyway, for surely it is the greater experience to step out of the proscenium frame and finally belong to what is left of oneself: and so belong to everyone and everything, and be deeply concerned?

I must get out of the past – I feel I want to start living *now* – a laughable wish at eighty, you will agree, but now, more than ever, anything seems possible. A few years ago, a major brush with my own possible extinction brought me great peace of mind. I had the salutary experience for a week, at least, of not knowing whether I had any more time to live. As I recovered from surgery, I felt I had been given a second chance to have open mind, open heart, open house. There is too much up-tightness behind closed doors, too much senile delinquency in non-acceptance, and I feel that growing older should be a great sum of addition. The subtraction is the certain and constantly surprising process of one's friends dying; getting stripped of them, like a tree of its leaves, and standing stark as the years go by. Not a pretty sight, but how joyous still to have a little adhering foliage . . .

I hate to finish this book – because I keep on suspecting some new adventure will come about: one that might have all the answers.

Index

Index

Index

Philip Ben Greet
lute your day
beau- ty when Ma-rie
Ma-rie Ma-rie Ma-rie
Ma-rie Tempest plays, Ma-rie Tem